은혜 위에 은혜

Grace Upon Grace

김수근 대성그룹 창업회장 회고록

Memoirs of Soo Keun Kim
Founding Chairman of the Daesung Group

대성그룹 창립 60주년 기념 출판

김수근 대성그룹 창업회장 회고록

은혜 위에 은혜

"우리가 다 그의 충만한데서 받으니
은혜 위에 은혜러라."
(요한복음 1:16)

JCR

Memoirs of Soo Keun Kim
Founding Chairman of the Daesung Group

Grace Upon Grace

"And from His fullness have we all received,
grace upon grace."
John 1:16 (RSV)

JCR

● 서 문

아버지의 회고록을 출간하면서…….

　　아버지께서는 자녀들과 대화하는 것을 매우 기뻐하셨다. 아버지의 말씀은 마치 향기로운 차와 같아서 항상 자녀들에게 깊은 감명을 주셨다.
　　자녀들이 아버지의 말씀을 좋아하는 것을 보시고 아버지께서는 우리들과 이야기하는 것을 무척이나 즐기셨다.
　　우리는 이러한 대화를 통해서 삶의 경륜과 지혜를 많이 배웠다. 아버지가 우리 자녀들에게 저녁마다 들려주셨던 아버지의 어린 시절과 대성그룹을 창업하시던 이야기는 한편의 감동적인 소설처럼 흥미진진했다.
　　그래서 나는 아버지가 우리에게 들려주신 대로 다음 세대에게 전해주는 것이 의미 있는 일이라고 생각하여 이렇게 아버지의 회고록을 편집하고 출판하게 되었다.
　　이 책을 읽는 독자마다 아버지의 생애를 읽으면서 반세기가 넘는 대성그룹의 역사 속에 드러나 있는 놀라우신 하나님의 은혜를 함께 발견하고 삶의 진실한 교훈과 지혜를 얻을 수 있기를 기도한다.

On the publication of the memoirs of my father...

Father took great joy in spending time talking with his children. His words were like the sweet aroma of tea, always inspirational and deeply moving. Recognizing how much we enjoyed listening to him speak, Father also enjoyed spending long moments with us.

We gained a great deal of wisdom through listening to his life experiences. The stories that he told us children every night about his childhood and about the Daesung Group's early days are fascinating and resemble the events of a touching novel. I find it worth retelling Father's stories to the present and following generations, and have decided to publish Father's memoirs as told to us by him long ago.

It is my earnest prayer that all who read this book about my father's life may discover God's amazing grace, with which He has blessed the Daesung Group for more than half a century, and that all may learn valuable lessons and gain true wisdom from the book.

여호와의 인자하심은 자기를 경외하는 자에게

영원부터 영원까지 이르며

그의 의는 자손의 자손에게 이르리니

곧 그의 언약을 지키고 그의 법도를 기억하여

행하는 자에게로다.

(시편 103:17-18)

2007년 5월 10일 대성그룹 창립 60주년을 맞이하며

연세대학교 교수 / 대성닷컴 사장

김정주 박사

[17]But from everlasting to everlasting
the LORD's love is with those who fear him,
and his righteousness with their children's children—
[18]with those who keep his covenant
and remember to obey his precepts.
(Psalm 103:17-18)

Dr. Jung Joo Kim
Professor, Yonsei University
President, Daesung.com
In celebration of the 60th anniversary of the Daesung Group
May 10, 2007

● 목 차

● *Contents*

Foreword

Chapter 1: The Years of My Youth • 13

    1. A Young Newspaper Boy and Man of the House
    2. Persistency Leads to Employment at Samguk Co., Ltd.
    3. A God Who Calls the Weak
    4. A Wedding Blessed by God
    5. My Studies in Japan
    6. Appointed Director of a Farmers' Bank

Chapter 2: The Beginning of the Daesung Group • 39

    1. The Briquette Business
    2. The Blackboard Manufacturing Business
    3. I Get Baptized and Quit Smoking
    4. The Weakest of the Weak Uplifted

Chapter 3: My Debut in Seoul • 57

    1. Starting the Briquette Business in Seoul
    2. Acquiring the Mungyeong Coal Mine
    3. The Seoul Briquette Factory a Groundbreaking Success
    4. Living at Don Am Jang

Chapter 4: A God Who is Near in Times of Hardship • 75

    1. Starting the Natural Gas Business
    2. Daegu Subway Construction Accident
    3. Details of the Gas Explosion
    4. God's Grace and Protection of the Gas Pipes
    5. Full-Scale Attack by the Media
    6. Courage in Faith
    7. Our Golden Wedding Anniversary, a 70th Birthday Celebration, and
       Younghoon's Wedding

Chapter 1
The Years of My Youth
나의
젊은 시절

대성그룹 창업주 김수근 회장의 84회 생신 잔치
The 84th birthday of the late founding Chairman of
the Daesung Group, Soo Keun Kim (2000)

약혼사진
Our engagement (1937)

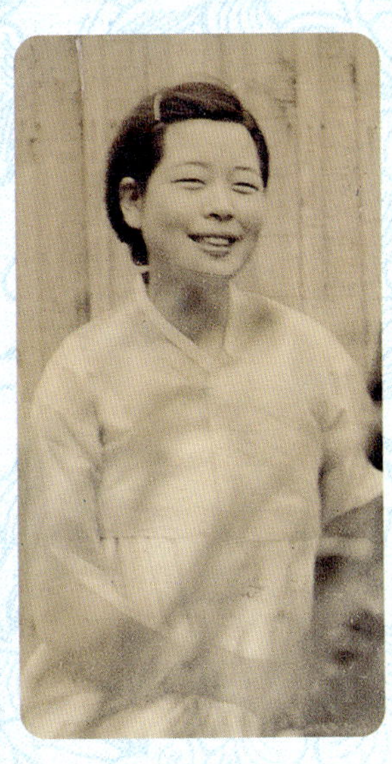

신혼사진
Newlyweds (1941)

1. 신문배달 하는 10세의 소년가장

　내가 한창 개구쟁이로 놀아야 할 초등학교 3학년 무렵에 아버지께서 갑자기 돌아가셨다. 아버지의 부재로 집이 순식간에 가난해지니, 새벽 4시에 신문 배달을 해야만 어머니와 두 남동생들을 먹여 살릴 수 있는 처지가 되었다. 당시 엄동설한의 대구에서 신발도 없이 맨발로 신문을 돌리던 내 삶에는 조금의 희망도 보이지 않았다. 소년가장으로 내게 주어진 짐이 너무 무거워서 나는 자살을 할까 생각하고 기차역에 가 보기도 했었다. 바로 그때 죽을 용기가 있으면 한번 살아보자는 각오가 조용히 내 마음에 들었다. 그래서 자살을 포기하고 용기를 내어 가난을 극복해 내려고 새롭게 마음을 가다듬었다. 자살의 길에서 나를 돌아서게 한 그 힘이 무엇이었는지 나는 그때 전혀 알지 못했지만……

　초등학교를 졸업하고 대구상업학교에 들어갔다. 다행이 어려운 환경에서도 공부를 곧잘 하는 편이어서 학교에서는 매번 좋은 성적으로 칭찬을 받았다. 신문배달을 하면서 공부를 하다 보니, 급기야 과로가 겹치면서 건강이 무척 안 좋아지게 되었다. 게다가 얼마 되지 않던 학비마저 마련하기가 여의치 않아 1년을 남겨두고 안타까운 마음이 가득했지만 학업을 중단할 수밖에 없었다.

1. A Young Newspaper Boy and Man of the House

When I was in the third grade, and when most children my age were busy having fun, my father passed away. His sudden death left our household poor and I found myself in a position where the survival of our family depended on my earnings. I had no choice but to get up every day at four o'clock in the morning to deliver newspapers. My life running newspaper routes in bare feet in the bone-chilling temperatures of winter in Daegu showed absolutely no signs of changing for the better. Taking on the responsibility of being the man of the house was so much of a burden to me that I even considered suicide. I managed to make my way to the train station, and just then, a thought entered my heart: *If I have the courage to die, I probably also have what it takes to live.* I gave up thoughts of suicide and turned away with a courageous heart, determined to overcome poverty. I had no idea then what power had turned me away from the path to suicide.

I successfully graduated from elementary school and enrolled at Daegu Commercial High School. Despite the difficult circumstances I faced, I received excellent grades and thus received many compliments, but because I had to juggle between my studies and running newspaper routes, I suffered from exhaustion and my health deteriorated. To make matters worse, I wasn't able to collect enough money to pay my tuition and, heartbroken and distressed because I only had one more year left, I withdrew from my studies.

2. 끈질긴 노력으로 얻은 삼국상회 일자리

조금 건강을 회복했을 때에도 여전히 생계가 막막해서 나는 일자리를 찾아야만 했다. 길을 지나다가 삼국상회라는 석탄회사의 대구 지사에서 사람을 채용한다는 공고를 보고 회사를 찾아갔다. 일본사람만 뽑는다고 했지만 내가 하도 끈질기게 일자리를 달라고 계속 부탁하니 결국 말단에 일자리를 하나 허락해 주었다. 나는 어렵게 얻은 직장에서 책임감을 가지고 부지런히 일했다. 외판, 경리, 그리고 얼마 후에는 주인집 아들의 가정교사까지 담당하게 되었다.

공부를 워낙 좋아했지만 어려운 가정형편으로 어쩔 수 없이 학업을 중단했기 때문에, 친구들이 학교에 갈 시간에 일하러 갈 때마다 나는 누구에게도 말할 수 없는 슬픔을 느끼곤 했다.

2. Persistency Leads to Employment at Samguk Co., Ltd.

I partially recovered my health and, though my options for making a living were as limited as before, I persisted in my efforts to find a job. I was strolling down the street one day when I stumbled upon a notice that the Daegu branch of a coal company called Samguk Co., Ltd., was hiring. When I arrived at their office, I was told that they were hiring only Japanese men. I pleaded with them over and over again until finally they gave in and gave me a job. Because it had been so difficult to get the job, I worked diligently and responsibly. I began with door-to-door sales. Later I was given accounting duties, and soon after, I was asked to be the owner's son's private tutor.

There was nothing I enjoyed more in the world than studying. I experienced unexpressible sadness whenever I headed to work while others headed to school.

3. 낮은 자를 부르시는 하나님

　어느 날 나는 누구도 전도하지 않았는데 삼국상회 건너편에 있는 칠성교회의 새벽기도에 나가게 되었다. 만약 아버지가 살아 계시던 시절의 부유한 형편이었다면 부잣집 아들인 나는 공부한답시고 교회를 찾지 않았을 것이다. 돌이켜 보면 내가 지극히 낮고 가난한 자리에서 어려움을 극복해 내려고 애썼던 시간은 전적으로 하나님의 은혜였다. 나를 한없이 낮추신 다음에 하나님은 나를 부르셨고, 하나님의 때에 지극히 높은 자리로 올리셨다. 내가 한국에서 가장 성공한 기업인 중의 한 사람으로 불리게 된 것은 전적으로 하나님의 은혜였다. 만약 나를 그냥 두셨다면, 아마 자그마한 가게를 운영하는 정도의 사람으로 일생을 살았을 것이다. 내가 가진 능력만으로는 큰 기업을 일으킬 수 없다는 것을 나는 잘 알고 있다.

　하나님께서 아브라함을 택하실 때 그는 모든 민족 중에 아주 작은 한 사람에 불과했다. 하나님께서는 왜 이런 작고 약한 자들을 택하실까? 하나님께서는 또한 택하신 자마다 연단을 통해서 하나님께서 쓰시기에 합당한 그릇으로 빚으신다. 요셉을 지극히 낮추시고 연단하신 후 애굽에서 총리대신이 되게 하신 것처럼 말이다.

　나를 부르셨을 때에도 내가 그보다 더 낮을 수 없을 만큼

3. A God Who Calls the Weak

One day, though I had not been subject to anyone's evangelistic efforts, I attended the early morning worship service at Chilsung Presbyterian Church, which stood across from Samguk Co. If I had continued to live the affluent life that I lived when my father was alive, I would have spent all my time immersed in my studies and would never have set foot in a church. Looking back, I realize that it was solely God's grace that allowed me to endure poverty and overcome my trials. God lowered me to the lowest level before He called me and, in His time, lifted me up high. I consider it wholly God's grace that led to my being named one of Korea's most successful businessmen. If He had abandoned me, I probably would have lived my life running a small shop, not knowing the great wonders of His grace. I know too well that it is not my skills or abilities alone that enabled me to establish a large enterprise.

Abraham was just one person from among the many peoples and nations of the world when God called him. Why does God purposely choose those who are weak and insignificant? God takes all whom He has chosen and shapes them into vessels that are worthy of His purpose, just as He chose Joseph when he had reached his lowest of lows and equipped him before elevating him to the position of prime

미천한 모습일 때였다. 일본강점기 때 한국의 작은 지방 도시인 대구에서 깜깜한 새벽부터 신문배달을 해야만 생계를 겨우 이어갈 수 있었다. 소년 가장이었던 17세 때부터는 일본인이 경영하는 삼국상회의 외판원으로 온갖 궂은일을 도맡아 해야만 했다. 이처럼 내가 가장 곤고했던 그때에 하나님께서 나를 부르셨다.

직장 건너편에 위치한 칠성교회 새벽예배에 3~4개월 다녀 보니, 목사님께서 하시는 말씀이 모두 유익하게 들렸다. 그래서 나는 과부로 외롭게 살아가시던 어머니께 교회에 나가 보시라고 말씀드렸다. 어머니를 모시고 간 곳은 집 근처에 있던 남산교회였다. 나를 그리스도 앞으로 부르신 하나님께서 얼마 후 나의 어머니도 믿음으로 부르신 것이다.

minister of Egypt.

God called me when I too could not sink any deeper. During the Japanese occupation, I had to deliver newspapers in the dark hours of the early morning in the small city of Daegu in order not to die. Left at a young age with the burden of being the man of the house, I worked for a Japanese-operated company as a salesman, enduring all kinds of hardship and humility at the youthful age of seventeen. God called me in my moment of greatest suffering.

Three to four months into my daily attendance at the early morning services at Chilsung Presbyterian Church, my ears opened up to the pastor's sermons and valuable teachings. Deeply moved, I suggested that my mother, who was living a rather lonely life as a widow, come to church with me. The two of us went to a nearby church, Namsan Presbyterian Church. God, who had called me to Christ, also called my mother, Grandma Kim, to a life of faith in Jesus Christ.

4. 하나님이 축복하신 결혼

내가 결혼한 곳이 바로 이 남산교회였다. 어머니의 교회 성경 공부 반 선생님은 최성연 권사님으로 장차 나의 장모님이 되실 분이었다. 원래 네 엄마에게는 경주의 최 부자 댁과 혼담이 오간 일이 있었다. 장모님은 외동딸이니만큼 인격 하나만 보고 시집을 보내야겠다고 하셨다. 대구에서 매우 가난했고 중학교도 못 마쳤지만, 내 인격을 귀하게 보시고 딸을 시집 보내려 하시니 친척들은 모두 반대했다. 네 엄마는 13세 때 예수님을 위해 순교하겠다고 헌신했고, 여학교를 졸업하기도 전에 그 어머니의 말씀에 순종하여 나와 약혼했다.

최성연 권사님은 새벽기도와 철야기도를 빠뜨리시지 않는 아주 신실한 분이셨다. 약혼 기간 중 어느 날 기도를 하시는데 "사위 공부 보내라."는 주님의 음성을 들으셨다고 했다. 그 말씀을 듣고 나는 그 자리에서 일본 유학을 결단하였다. 나의 어머니를 간곡하게 설득하여 동의를 받아낸 후, 뼈에 사무치도록 하고 싶던 공부를 다시 시작하기 위해 곧바로 일본으로 떠났다. 네 엄마는 여학교 졸업 후에 평양여자신학교에 들어갔다. 그 후 신사참배로 학교가 폐교되어 돌아와서는 4년 약혼 기간의 대부분의 시간을 교회에서 가난한 문맹들을 가르치는 일에 봉사했다.

4. A Wedding Blessed by God

I was married at Namsan Presbyterian Church. The Bible study groups at the church were taught by Elder Sung Nyun Choi, Grandma Yeu, who later became my mother-in-law. Originally, marriage arrangements between your mother and a man from a well-to-do household in Gyeongju were being made. Grandma Yeu wanted to find a good-natured man, rather than a wealthy man, for her only daughter. I was probably the poorest man in Daegu and had not even graduated from junior high school, yet Grandma Yeu placed great value on my character and gave me your mother's hand in marriage. Rightfully so, your mother's relatives objected. At the age of thirteen, your mother offered to sacrifice her life to martyrdom, but remaining obedient as always to her mother's instruction, your mother got engaged to me even before she graduated from high school.

Grandma Yeu was a devout Christian. Never once had she missed a prayer meeting or early morning prayer service. While your mother and I were still engaged, Grandma Yeu heard the voice of God speak: "Send your son-in-law abroad to study." Immediately, it was decided that I would go to Japan and study. After much earnest effort, I received Grandma Kim's permission to go. For too long I had hoped, with a desire that cut through my bones, to continue my

　　1941년 10월 27일 맑은 가을날, 유학 중에 잠시 귀국하여 나는 네 엄마와 결혼했다. 당시 여학교를 졸업한 사람들은 모두 금반지를 결혼선물로 받았지만 가난한 고학생과 결혼한 네 엄마는 은반지를 받았고 신혼여행은 꿈도 꿀 수 없었다.

　　키가 컸던 네 엄마는 허리를 펴지 못할 만큼 낮은 집에서 3년 동안 시어머니의 대소변을 받아내면서도 불평하거나 얼굴 한번 찌푸린 적이 없었다. 항상 환하게 웃으면서 찬양과 기도, 사랑과 은혜로 병중의 시어머니를 극진하게 간호했다. 네 엄마의 헌신적인 사랑은 바위보다도 더 단단하게 닫혀있던 친척들의 마음을 서서히 녹여갔고, 나와 어머니밖에는 아무도 믿지 않던 우리 가족들을 마침내 하나님 앞으로 모두 나오게 만들었다.

studies. I left for Japan right away. In the meantime, your mother graduated from high school and entered Pyeongyang Woman's Theological Seminary. Unfortunately, the institution was closed because of its resistance to the harsh enforcement of Shinto worship by Japanese authorities, and your mother spent the next three and a half long years of engagement teaching poor, illiterate people at church.

I returned to Korea briefly, and one clear autumn day, October 27, 1941, I married your mother. In those days, all women who had graduated from high school received gold wedding rings, but because I was a poor student, I could only afford a silver ring for your mother; and there was no way we could even dream of going on a honeymoon.

Your mother was quite tall, so living in a low-ceiling house made it difficult to walk around without having to hunch her back. For three years, your mother took care of Grandma Kim in that house. Never once did she make a face or complain about tending to your grandma's bathroom needs. Your mother always had a bright smile on her face and looked after her mother-in-law with a devoted heart, prayer, love, and grace. Your mother's devotion slowly but surely softened the rock-solid hearts of our relatives, bringing every last one of them to God.

5. 일본 유학 생활

말씀에 순종하여 떠난 일본 유학 생활은 결코 쉬운 시간이
아니었다. 나는 중학교 과정을 마치지 못했기 때문에 저녁에
는 중학교 과정을, 낮에는 대학교 과정을 공부해야만 했다. 그
런 어려운 조건을 참고 공부하면서 3년 만에 일본대학을 수석
으로 졸업할 수 있었다. 약소국인 한국에서 온 청년이라고 무
시하던 일본대학 교수들은 놀라움을 금치 못했다. 담당교수
한 분은 내가 강의를 꼼꼼히 기록하는 것을 눈여겨 보다가 자
신의 책을 출판하는 데 내 노트가 꼭 필요하다고 했다. 어릴
적에 아버지로부터 명필이라고 칭찬을 받곤 했는데 일본대학
에 와서 확인된 셈이다.

내가 대학 졸업을 앞두고 있던 시기에 갑작스레 한국에서
'어머니 위독' 이라는 전보가 왔다. 그 소식을 듣자 마음이 얼
마나 급했던지 속히 귀국해야 한다는 생각밖에 없었다. 다행
스럽게도 귀국한 후에는 위중하시던 어머니께서는 차츰 나아
가셨다.

하지만 고학생활의 어려움 속에서 공부를 계속하다 보니
다시 내 건강이 극도로 나빠져서 결핵을 앓게 되었다. 그 상황
을 알고도 결혼한 네 엄마는 지극한 사랑과 기도로 나를 돌보
아 주었다. "내 몸의 피를 다 쏟더라도 남편의 건강이 회복된

5. My Studies in Japan

I left for Japan in obedience to the voice of God, but my life in Japan was not without its share of hardship. Because I had not completed junior high school, I spent my evenings studying through the junior high school curriculum, while during the day I immersed myself in my university studies. I patiently endured the overwhelmingly long hours of study and, within three years, graduated at the top of the class. The professors at the Japanese university could not hide their amazement in seeing me, whom they had mocked and regarded as no more than a young man from a weak country, rise to the top. Remembering how I would take excellent notes during lectures, my supervising professor told me how my notes were imperative to the publishing of his latest book. Ever since I was a little boy, my father had told me I had excellent handwriting skills. His words were verified in Japan.

At about the time of my graduation, I received a telegram from Korea that my mother was in critical condition. Upon receiving the news, my heart raced and I panicked. The only thought I had in my head was that I had to leave immediately, so I did. Fortunately, Grandma Kim slowly began to recover after my return.

My devotion to my studies, combined with the fact that I

다면 기쁘게 죽겠습니다."라고 매일 네 엄마가 기도하면서 정성껏 돌봐 준 덕분에 나는 몇 년 지나지 않아 건강을 완전히 회복하게 되었다. 당시에 결핵은 걸리면 죽게 되는 중병이었다. 네 엄마의 생명을 내어놓은 간절한 기도를 하나님이 들어주셔서 나의 생명을 살려 주신 것이다.

돌이켜 볼 때 나는 하나님의 사랑을 받을 자격이 전혀 없는 사람이었다. 왜 내게 그런 큰 은혜를 내려주셨는지 알지 못했고 그 은혜를 깨닫는 데 영적으로 많이 둔감하였다. 죄인을 불러 회개시키시고 십자가에서 흘리신 피로 씻어주시어 영혼뿐만 아니라 육신까지도 온전케 하시는 그 사랑을 뒤늦게 깨달았으니 어떻게 다 감사해야 할지 모르겠구나.

was a self-supporting student, caused my physical health to grow weak. My lungs began to show signs of tuberculosis, and it turned out that I actually had contracted the disease. At the time, tuberculosis was an incurable disease that meant certain death once contracted. Despite my illness, your mother willingly married me and looked after me with love and heartfelt prayers. "Even if all my blood were to pour out and I were to die, if only my husband could recover, I would die joyfully," your mother would daily pray. I fully recovered after a few years, and I owe it to your mother's sincere care. God heard your mother's earnest prayers and saw how she was ready to sacrifice her life for her dying husband; and He spared my life.

Reflecting back, I realize that I am by no means worthy of God's abundant love. I was spiritually oblivious to God's grace. For what reason had He shown me such unfathomable grace? I wondered. He called me, a sinner, to repentance; He cleansed me of my sins with the blood that His only Son shed on the cross; and He healed not only my soul but also my physical body. No words can ever express how grateful I am for God s unconditional love and His saving grace.

6. 금융조합 이사가 되다

졸업 후 나는 직장을 찾던 중에 금융조합 이사 시험에 응시하게 되었다. 얼마 후 내가 그 시험에 수석으로 합격했다는 통지를 받았다. 이 소식은 병상에 계시던 어머니께 생전에 큰 위로가 되었다.

요즘의 농업협동조합 지점장과 같은 직책인 금융조합 이사는 당시에 관사에서 지냈는데 발령을 받고 가보니, 천 평이 넘는 부지의 뜰에 청포도가 주렁주렁 열려 있고, 마당에는 갖가지 푸른 채소가 싱싱하게 자라고 있었다. 네 엄마는 이렇게 좋은 환경을 주신 하나님께 감사드리며 매우 행복해하는 모습이었다.

금융조합 직원들과 동네 유지 분들은 젊은 내게 깍듯이 어른 대접을 해주었다. 그 후 농촌을 둘러보니 농민들의 생활은 말할 수 없이 피폐해 있었다. 나는 일제 당국이 우리 농민들에게서 불법적으로 차출한 소들을 찾아주고 낮은 이자로 대출해주는 방식으로 그들이 소작농에서 자작농으로 살도록 도와주었다. 고통 중에 있던 농민들이 새로운 삶의 터전을 찾을 수 있도록 조금이라도 도울 수 있었던 것은 당시 내게 매우 큰 기쁨이었다.

부르시고 복을 주심으로 내 삶에는 참으로 많은 기적이 일

6. Appointed Director of a Farmers' Bank

Upon returning to Korea from Japan and in the midst of searching for a job, I decided to take a bankers' exam to apply for the position of director at a bank. I soon received notice that I had passed the examinations with the highest results. This news brought great joy to Grandma Kim, who was still very ill.

The status of a director at a Farmers' Bank in those days was equivalent to that of today's manager of an agricultural association. The director of a Farmers' Bank was always provided with a private residence. The house we were provided with stood on 1,000 *pyeong* (3,300 square meters) of land with vines hanging with plump clusters of grapes and a garden of fresh vegetables. Your mother was absolutely thrilled and filled with thanksgiving for the beauty that stood before her eyes.

The employees at the Farmers' Bank and the elders in the neighborhood treated me, though I was quite young, with respect and dignity because I was the bank director. In observing the people of this farming village and the lives of the farmers, I noted that the level of poverty was high. I did all that I could do in my capacity as the director of the Farmers' Bank to return to the farmers the cows that had been unjustly stolen away by Japanese authorities. And by making low-interest loans available to the farmers, I helped change their status from tenants to owners of farmland. Just the simple fact

어났다. 말할 수 없이 궁핍했던 고학생이 3년 만에 중학교와 대학교 과정을 졸업한 것도 놀라운데, 현숙한 아내를 만나 믿음의 가정까지 이루게 되었으니 말이다. 그와 함께 당시에 한국 사람들이 가장 선망했던 금융조합 이사직에 오를 수 있게 해주셨다. 하나님의 말씀을 좇아간 후, 전에는 조금도 희망이 보이지 않던 내게 이렇게 큰 변화가 일어난 것이다.

내가 가장 좋아하는 찬양이 찬송가 360장이다. 평생 베풀어주신 하나님의 극진하신 은혜에 부족하게나마 감사하며 동행하고자 했던 나의 마음을 잘 표현하고 있다.

예수 나를 오라 하네.
예수 나를 오라 하네.
어디든지 주를 따라
주와 같이 같이 가려네.

주의 인도하심 따라
주의 인도하심 따라
어디든지 주를 따라
주와 같이 같이 가려네.
(찬송가 360장)

that I could be of assistance to the suffering farmers, helping them find new hope, brought me great joy and happiness.

After receiving God's call, and because of His countless blessings, I began to witness many miracles. The fact that I, a poor self-supporting student, was able to complete the junior high school curriculum and graduate from university within three years is a miracle in itself. Yet He also provided me with a virtuous wife and allowed me to be the head of a God-loving, God-fearing family. On top of that, God made it possible for me to rise to what was then a most highly regarded position in Korean society—director of a Farmers' Bank. I, who had once lived without a hint of hope, was now experiencing great change since following God's Word. Hymn 360 is my favorite hymn, for it expresses, though only in part, my yearning desire to follow Christ and my grateful heart for the amazing grace that God has poured on me throughout my life.

Where He Leads Me (Hymn #360)

(verse 1)
I can hear my Saviour calling,
I can hear my Saviour calling,
I can hear my Saviour calling,
"Take thy cross and follow, follow Me."

예수님께서 나를 부르신 후 내게 일어난 일들은 모든 것이 한마디로 은혜 위에 은혜였다. 내가 한 것이 아니라 전적으로 하나님께서 주신 선물이었다.

The events that occurred in my life since the day I was called to Jesus were, to say it simply in one phrase, a work of God's *Grace Upon Grace*. The Grace He poured on me was not given because of any good deeds of my own but solely as a gift.

Chapter 2

The Beginning of
the Daesung Group

대성그룹의
시작

1960년대 칠성동 대성연탄 공장
The Daesung Briquette Factory in Chilseong (1960s)

대성산업 창립15주년
15th Anniversary of Daesung
Industrial Corporation (1962)

1960년대 임직원들
With employees (1960s)

1960년대 광산 방문
Visit to the coal mine (1960s)

광산 방문
Visit to the coal mine (1982)

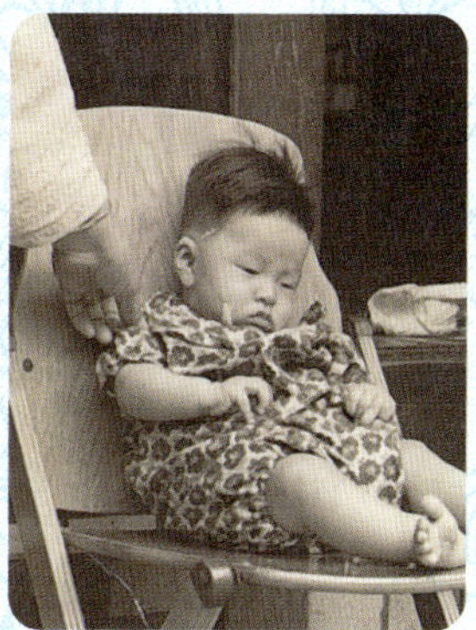

김영훈 회장 돌 사진
Younghoon's 1st birthday

일본 첫 방문
First excursion to Japan (1958)

대구 남성로 집
Our home in Namsung-ro, Daegu (1956)

대구에서
In Daegu (mid-1950s)

대구상고 야구단
The Daegu Commercial High School
baseball team (1975)

1. 연탄사업 시작

3년 간 금융조합 이사 생활을 하고 나자 해방이 되었다. 그 감격을 어떻게 다 표현할 수 있을까. 하지만 안타깝게도 해방을 맞은 기쁨과 동시에 한국은 사회적으로 큰 혼란에 빠지는 상황을 겪게 되었다. 무엇보다도 인플레가 심하여 한달 월급으로는 며칠을 버티기가 힘든 지경이었다. 나는 동생의 결혼과 해방 후 귀국한 누님 가족의 부양, 그리고 자녀들 교육을 생각하니 당시 월급으로는 도저히 감당이 되지 않았다. 결국 많은 고심 끝에 사업을 시작해야겠다고 결심했다.

영천금융조합에서 최선을 다해 일한 결과로 조합이 어느 정도 안정되어 원활하게 운영되자 상주금융조합으로 발령이 났다. 그곳은 큰 소요가 일어나서 정상화를 이루기까지 매우 힘든 곳이었다. 나는 이 기회에 사표를 내기로 했다. 많은 반대가 있었지만 사정을 충분히 설명하자 내 사표는 마침내 수리되었다.

해방 직후 한국 경제는 매우 어려웠다. 나는 삼국상회에서 일한 경험을 살려서 익숙했던 연탄제조업을 시작했다. 1947년 5월 10일, 처음 새벽기도를 드렸던 대구 칠성동에 50평 정도의 땅을 사서 서기 한 사람과 일꾼 한 사람을 데리고 연탄공장을 시작했다. 네 엄마는 사업이 크게 성공하기를 바라면서

1. The Briquette Business

Three years into my term of office as director at the Farmers' Bank, Korea won liberation from Japanese colonialism. No words could even begin to express the deep emotions we felt. Liberation brought Korea great joy and relief, but at the same time, it also brought about social disorder. Above all, inflation rates were so high that it was nearly impossible to survive more than a few days on a month's salary. My salary was nowhere near sufficient to pay for my younger brother's wedding, to support my older sister's family, which was returning to Korea, or to pay for my children's education. After careful consideration, I decided to set up my own business.

Working diligently, I raised the Yeongcheon Farmers' Bank to a stable position and, because the bank was operating quite smoothly, it was decided that I would be transferred to the Sangju Farmers' Bank, which was experiencing difficulties beyond control. I saw this as a chance to resign from my position. Though there was much opposition to my resignation at first, after I explained my family situation, my letter of resignation was processed.

After the liberation, the Korean economy suffered greatly. With my past experience working for Samguk Co., I decided to start my very own coal-briquette manufacturing company. On May 10, 1947, I bought a 50-*pyeong* (165 square meters) area of land in the Chilseong area in Daegu where I had

회사 이름을 '대성(大成)'이라고 지어 주었다. 이것이 바로 대성그룹의 시작이다.

대성그룹 창립기념일이 네 엄마의 생신과 같은 날인 5월 10일이 된 것은 우연이 아니다. 대성그룹이 지금까지 받고 있는 많은 축복은 하나님께서 모두 네 엄마의 믿음을 보시고 허락하신 아브라함의 복이다. 나는 우리 후손들이 모두 그리스도를 잘 믿고 아브라함의 복을 받음으로 대성그룹이 계속 하나님께서 복 주시는 기업으로 이어져가기를 소망한다.

주변 사람들은 일본에 유학하여 대학도 나오고 금융조합 이사까지 지낸 사람이 고작 작은 연탄회사를 사업이라고 시작한다며 조롱 섞인 눈빛으로 나를 보곤 했다. 하지만 금융조합 이사로 일하는 동안 원칙과 소신을 지켜온 결과, 수중에 돈이 없어 전적으로 대출을 받아 시작한 연탄제조업에 대해 나와 네 엄마는 진심으로 감사한 마음으로 일을 추진해 갔다. 나는 하나님께 맡기는 마음으로 사업을 경영하면서 점차 확장해갈 수 있는 방법을 깊이 고심하였다.

attended my first ever early morning service at church. I hired two employees—a secretary and a laborer—and started a briquette factory. Your mother, full of hope and great expectations for the business, named the company Daesung—*dae* (great) and *sung* (success). And thus began the history of the Daesung Group.

It is no coincidence that the Daesung Group was founded on your mother's birthday, May 10. The countless blessings that the Daesung Group continues to reap to this day is the blessing of Abraham that God lovingly bestowed because of your mother's display of faith in Him. I earnestly hope and pray that my descendants may press on in faith, and that, through receiving the blessing of Abraham, the Daesung Group will continue to prosper.

I had studied abroad in Japan and graduated from university. I had even been appointed director of a Farmers' Bank. And there I was, setting up a small-scale briquette factory. Eyes of ridicule surrounded me. When I was serving as director at the Farmers' Bank, I did not give in to bribes, nor did I ever forego my integrity. As a result, I had no savings, but strangely enough, your mother and I were sincerely grateful, for we were able to open up the briquette factory with a bank loan. I operated the business with a heart of thanksgiving, leaving everything in God's hand, and I gradually began to expand the business.

2. 칠판공장 시작

그러던 어느 날 네 엄마가 불쑥 칠판공장을 하면 어떻겠느냐고 물었다. 당시 남산교회 소사로 있으면서 무척 어렵게 살았던 한 부인이 있었다. 그 남편이 칠판기술자라는 것을 알고 네 엄마는 그 부인에게 물어 보았다. 기술자라면 잘 살 텐데 왜 이렇게 못 사느냐고 말이다. 남편이 정직하지 않아서 늘 빈곤하다는 말을 들었다. 네 엄마는 그 젊은 부인이 측은하여 그 남편이 정직하지 못한 사람이란 얘기는 내게 꺼내지 않았다. 그대로 말하면 내가 채용하지 않았을 것을 잘 알았기 때문이다. 그 칠판기술자를 채용하여 칠판을 많이 만들어 창고에 가득 채우고 납품을 기다리던 시기에 6·25사변이 터지고 말았다. 나는 너희들을 데리고 부산으로 피난을 갔다. 맥아더 장군의 인천상륙작전이 성공하여 서울이 수복되었다는 소식을 듣고서 나는 가족들을 데리고 대구로 올라왔다.

전쟁 통에 남은 것이라고는 창고에 가득 채워 두었던 칠판뿐이었다. '보통 때나 칠판을 사지, 전쟁 한복판에 누가 칠판을 사겠는가?' 하고 한숨을 쉬며 경상북도 도청 앞을 지나는데, 놀라운 광고가 크게 붙어있는 것을 보았다. '칠! 판! 구! 함!' 사정을 알아보았다. 전쟁 중에 북한군들이 군대를 주둔시킬 넓은 집을 찾다 보니 학교밖에 없었다. 초등학교, 중고등학

2. The Blackboard Manufacturing Business

One day out of the blue, your mother made a suggestion to set up a blackboard manufacturing business. She knew of a poor married woman who was a proctor at Namsan Presbyterian Church. Your mother had heard that the woman's husband was a skillful manufacturer of blackboards. Unsure as to why the woman was so poor when her husband was a skilled man, your mother asked her why this was so. The woman told your mother that they lived in poverty because her husband was a dishonest man who was not trusted by his employers. Your mother felt so much compassion towards the woman that she did not disclose to me the fact that the husband was a dishonest man. She knew too well that I probably would not have hired the man if I had known. Nevertheless, the man was hired and our storage room soon filled up with blackboards. Just when we were ready to distribute the goods, the Korean War broke out. I took all of you my children and together we fled to Busan for safety. Later, on hearing that U.S. Army General Douglas MacArthur had successfully landed at Incheon and that Seoul had been regained, our family returned home to Daegu.

Nothing had been left untouched by the war except the stacks of blackboards we had locked up in the storage room. I thought to myself, *Who in their right mind would buy a*

교, 대학교 등 학교마다 들어가 군대를 주둔시킨 북한군은 밥을 짓고 추위를 피하기 위해 칠판을 불쏘시개로 다 써버렸다. 서울 수복 후 전국적으로 학교수업을 다시 시작하면서, 교육당국은 칠판을 구하기 위해 고군분투하고 있었다. 그때 우리 창고에 가득 차있던 칠판과 남아있는 재료로 만든 모든 칠판은 순식간에 팔려 나갔다. 그 결과로 적잖은 자본을 얻게 되어 나는 연탄공장을 계속 확장시켜 나갈 수 있었다.

blackboard in the middle of a war? Discouraged, I sighed as I walked by the Gyeongsangbuk-do Provincial Government building, when my eyes beheld a large notice that read: "COLLECTING BLACKBOARDS." I looked into it. During the war, the North Korean soldiers had looked for large spaces to station their men. They happened to use elementary and high school buildings and even university campuses to station the Red Army. By the end of the war, the soldiers had used up all the blackboards in schools throughout the south to make fires to cook food and keep themselves warm. After Seoul was regained, schools throughout the country began to reopen. The Ministry of Education was searching hard to gather blackboards for all the schools. All the blackboards in our factory, and all the blackboards we managed to produce with the left-over raw materials, sold out in the blink of an eye. And with the money we collected from blackboard sales, I was able to expand our briquette business.

3. 세례를 받고 담배를 끊다

이렇게 받은 은혜가 많음에도 불구하고 나는 마음으로 하나님을 온전히 섬기지 못했고 담배마저 많이 피우고 있었다. 네 엄마의 기도를 들으신 하나님께서 나를 가만히 두지 않으셨다. 언젠가부터 나는 기침이 너무 심하여서 병원을 찾아갔다. 기관지염에 걸렸다고 진단한 의사는 내게 경고했다. 이대로 담배를 피우면 오래 살지 못할 것이라고 말이다. 그때 내 마음에 '내가 일하러 세상에 났지, 담배 피우러 왔나?' 하는 생각이 들어 그날로 바로 담배를 끊었다. 하루에 세 갑을 피우던 내가 갑자기 담배를 끊으니 주변에서 다들 놀라워했다. 이것은 모두 바로 네 엄마와 가족들의 뜨거운 기도에 대한 하나님의 응답이었다.

6·25 직후 나는 세례를 받았다. 영훈이가 유아 세례를 받은 바로 그 뜻 깊은 날이었다. 하나님께서 베풀어주신 은혜가 매우 커서 감사함으로 그리스도를 믿는 믿음을 하나님과 교회 앞에서 고백했다. 내가 세례를 받기까지 네 엄마는 나를 위해 참으로 오랫동안 무릎 꿇고 하나님께 기도드린 것을 잘 알고 있다. 하나님의 은혜를 받을 자격이 전혀 없는 죄인의 괴수인 내게 베풀어주신 그 한량없는 사랑을 너무나도 늦게 깨달았다. 오래 참으시고 기다려주신 하나님의 크신 사랑을 그 무엇으로도 표현할 길이 없구나.

3. I Get Baptized and Quit Smoking

God had poured His grace upon me, yet I continued to smoke and only half-heartedly follow Him. But because God had been listening to your mother's earnest prayers, He did not forsake me. One day my cough became so severe that I went to see a doctor. I was told that I had contracted bronchitis and was warned that if I continued to smoke, I wouldn't live long. My heart thought, *I was born to work, not to smoke.* And from that day forward, I quit smoking for good. Everyone was so amazed to see me, a man who smoked three packs of cigarettes daily, quit smoking in an instant. Without a doubt, this miracle was God's answer to the heartfelt prayers that your mother and our family prayed.

Immediately after the Korean War and on the same day Younghoon was baptized, I too was baptized. I was so grateful for the unfathomable grace that God bestowed upon me that my heart was led to declare my faith in Christ before God and the entire congregation. I know that your mother had for so long knelt before God in prayer for my redemption, and it was her prayers and God's amazing grace that led to my baptism. All along, God's infinite love had embraced me, a man nowhere near worthy of His grace, but I did not recognize it until then. No words of mine can ever express God's amazing grace that patiently waited for me.

4. 지극히 작은 자 하나에게 한 것

네 엄마가 가난한 부인 한 사람을 도우려고 그 남편을 채용하게 한 것이 이렇게 우리에게 큰 복이 되었다. 하나님께서 사람에게 복을 주실 때는 상황에 관계없이 복을 주신다. 한국이 가장 가난했고 전쟁으로 심히 열악한 환경에서 정직하지 못한 사람을 데리고 일을 했으니, 이보다 더 어려운 조건이 어디 있겠는가! 그러나 모든 악조건에도 불구하고 하나님께서 우리 가정과 우리 기업에 말할 수 없는 복을 주셨다. 하나님의 은혜는 하늘보다 넓고 바다보다 깊다는 것을 명심하길 바란다.

이 경험을 바탕으로 나는 평안한 마음으로 사업을 진행해 갔다. 6·25 직후에 비해 한국의 국민소득은 지금 천 배에 가깝게 성장했다. 평화로운 시대를 맞이했고 유능하고 성실한 사람들이 많아지게 되었다. 하나님께서 앞으로 너희에게 엄청나게 큰 복을 주실 것이다. 그리스도 안에서 모든 믿는 자에게 약속하신 아브라함의 복은 부채와 나팔 같다. 너희를 향하신 축복이 이제 막 시작되었다. 나팔을 불면 소리가 널리 퍼지고

4. The Weakest of the Weak Uplifted

[40] *"The King will reply, 'I tell you the truth,
whatever you did for one of the least of these
brothers of mine, you did for me.' "
(Matthew 25:40)*

Your mother's desire to help out a poor woman and give a dishonest man a job, in the end, paved the pathway to greater blessings. When God blesses man, He does so regardless of situations and circumstances. I tell you, I don't think anything could have made situations worse for us; after all, we had already hired a dishonest man and Korea was in its most impoverished state, struggling to recover from a devastating war. Despite our dire circumstances, God showered down countless blessings on our family and business. Indeed, God's grace is wider than the skies and deeper than the oceans, never forget.

God's grace was and is sufficient. I was able to carry out my business with peace in my heart. Korea's current national per-capita income has grown nearly a thousand-fold since the end of the Korean War (1950-1953). Korea now welcomes a peaceful era and the number of honest, competent people has increased as well. God will continue to pour even greater blessings on you, my children. The blessing of Abraham,

부채를 펴면 살이 넓게 펼쳐지듯, 앞으로 너희와 대성그룹이 받을 복은 이제까지 받은 어떠한 복보다도 클 것이다. 지금까지 대성그룹을 축복하신 하나님께서 앞으로 너희에게 그리스도 안에서 복을 주시면 너희는 오대양 육대주를 주님께 돌이키게 하는 데까지 나아갈 것이다.

which God promised to all who are faithful, is like a trumpet and fan. You are now only beginning to experience the endless blessings God has in store for you. Just as sound from a trumpet's blow travels wide and as a fan unfolds and spreads wide, I know the blessings which God has so far poured on us will travel wide and fan out to bring even greater blessings on you and the Daesung Group. I know He will continue to bless you, my children, in Christ Jesus and use you to bring the five oceans and six continents to Him.

Chapter 3
My Debut in Seoul
나의
서울 진출

서울 관철동 사무실
Office in Gwancheol-
dong, Seoul (1970)

대성창립 30주년
Celebrating Daesung's 30th
Anniversary (1977)

전경련 남미 순방
Visit to South America (1975)

전경련 아프리카 순방
Visit to Africa with the
members of the Federation of
Korean Industries (1979)

독일 지멘스 공장 및 본사 방문
Visit to Siemens factory and office in Germany (1994)

은혼식
Our silver wedding (1972)

스노베 일본 대사 돈암장 방문
Japanese Ambassador Snobe's visit
to Don Am Jang (1979)

돈암장 여름
Don Am Jang (Summer 1963)

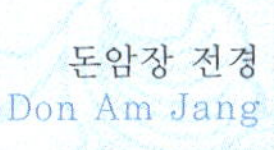

김수근 창업회장 회갑연
My 60th birthday celebration (1976)

돈암장 전경
Don Am Jang

1. 서울에서 연탄사업 시작

대구에서 연탄공장을 계속 확장하여 매출이 크게 증대되자 자연스럽게 서울로 진출하고 싶은 마음이 강하게 일어났다. 마침 서울 왕십리에 큰 연탄공장 하나가 시장에 매물로 나왔다. 이 공장 주인은 6·25 직후 파손된 공장을 수리하여 연탄사업을 하다가 크게 부도가 나서 어려운 상황에 있었다. 1958년 나는 왕십리의 그 공장을 샀는데, 내게 회사를 판 사람의 직원 한 사람이 부정직하게 나왔다. 잔금을 다 치렀음에도 트집을 잡아 번번이 나를 괴롭혀서 그 후 몇 년 동안 심한 마음고생을 하게 만들었다. 다행이 법을 전공한 것이 그때 내게 많은 도움이 되었다. 법적으로 적절하게 대응한 결과 모든 재판에서 승소하여 당시의 어려움을 해결할 수 있었다. 공의와 인자로 다스리시는 하나님의 은혜였다고 생각한다.

1. Starting the Briquette Business in Seoul

As we continued to expand our briquette factory in Daegu, sales continued to grow, and naturally I developed the desire to expand the business to Seoul. The opportunity to do so presented itself when a large briquette factory in Wangsimni came out on the market. The owner of the factory renovated it because it had been destroyed in the war, but soon after he began to operate a briquette business, he went bankrupt, leaving him in a difficult situation. I justly and lawfully bought that factory in 1958, but one of the previous owner's employees made some dishonest accusations. All transactions were complete, but the man falsely claimed that I had not paid the amount due. For years after that, I endured his harassment. Having majored in law, my background helped me win the case before the Supreme Court. All this I owe to God, who delights in what is just and true.

2. 문경광산 인수

곧이어 연탄공장에 제일 필요한 원료인 석탄을 원활하게
수급하기 위해 광산사업을 시작하였다. 1960년에 문경광산을
인수했는데, 탄질이 낮고 광맥이 깊어서 수익성이 없다는 판
단으로 거의 포기한 광산이었다. 나는 낙후된 문경광산을 기
계화하고 많은 노력과 시간을 들인 끝에 드디어 수익을 내도
록 변화시켜 갔다. 그 후 복지시설을 확충하고 광산 한복판에
교회를 세워 함께 예배를 드릴 수 있는 공간을 마련했다.

1970년대 말, 석탄사업이 사양사업이 되면서 동시에 일어
난 광부들의 소요로 광산들이 하나 둘씩 폐광하게 되었다. 문
경광산도 폐광 절차를 밟았다. 그때 나는 문경의 직원들이 각
각 적성에 맞는 대성그룹 계열사의 희망 직종에서 일할 수 있
도록 배려했다. 직원들과 그들의 가정은 어려움 속에서도 절
망하지 않도록 해준 회사에 대해 더욱 충실한 마음으로 업무
에 임하고 보답해 주어 도리어 내가 더욱 감사했다.

문경광산 가까운 곳에 문경세재와 주흘산이 있다. 주흘산
이 경매에 나오게 되자 나는 입찰에 적극 임했다. 함께 경쟁하
던 사람이 입찰 예정시간에 도착하지 않아 내게 낙찰이 되었
다. 얼마 후 도착한 그 사람은 차가 긁히는 가벼운 교통사고로
늦었다고 오히려 사과를 전해왔다. 나는 주흘산에 열심히 조

2. Acquiring the Mungyeong Coal Mine

Coal is the raw material in greatest demand in the briquette business. In order to ensure a regular supply of coal for our briquette factory, I decided to enter the coal mine industry and buy a coal mine. I took over the Mungyeong Coal Mine in 1960. Hardly anyone showed interest in this coal mine, for its minerals were buried deep underground and were of low quality. Many deemed it a poor investment. Nevertheless, I bought it and incorporated coal-mining mechanization technologies and, after dedicating much time and effort to the coal mine, we began to reap profits. Soon after, we constructed recreation centers on the land and later erected a church at the center, creating a space for people to worship together.

In the late 1970s, coal increasingly became a declining industry and miners' demonstrations began to escalate. Coal mines began to close one after another. The Mungyeong Coal Mine also closed down, but I made arrangements for its employees to fill positions in various subsidiaries of the Daesung Group. When I look back, I am more grateful to my employees and their families than they to me, for in return, they assumed all duties and responsibilities with a great sense of loyalty to the company.

The Mungyeong Pass and Mt. Juheul are near the

림사업을 하여 울창한 숲을 만들었다. 후손들에게 맑고 푸른 환경을 물려주고 싶은 꿈이 이루어진 것이다. 네 엄마는 주흘산에 국제적인 선교훈련원과 세계적인 기독교육기관을 지어 세계선교에 크게 쓰임 받는 거룩한 곳이 되도록 기도하고 있는데 하나님 뜻대로 응답되기를 바란다.

Mungyeong Coal Mine. Mt. Juheul, which was the last remaining property of the royal family of the Joseon Dynasty, was put up for public bidding. The competing bidder did not show up at the arranged time and place, so my bid was accepted. Moments later, the competing bidder arrived, apologizing for being late as he had gotten into a minor traffic accident on his way there.

As a result of various forestation efforts, a thick grove of trees now stands on Mt. Juheul. I feel that my dream of leaving my descendants an inheritance of a clean, green environment has come true. Your mother continues to pray that the international missionary training center and global Christian education foundation she wishes to found may one day stand there for global missions. I hope that God will answer her prayers, according to His perfect plan.

3. 크게 성공한 서울의 연탄공장

내가 처음 서울에 진출한 1958년만해도 산에서 나무를 잘라 불을 때는 집들이 많았다. 장작보다 훨씬 편리한 연탄이 생산되자, 많은 사람들이 연탄공장에 몰려와서 연탄을 사가지고 갔다. 회사의 매출은 놀랍도록 크게 성장하였다. 그리고 서울에서 연탄공장을 수리하여 가동을 개시한 바로 그때, 박정희 대통령은 산림 녹화정책을 발표했다. 이전까지는 산에서 나무를 잘라서 연료로 사용하는 것이 허용되었으나, 녹화정책이 발표된 후부터 입산금지령이 내려졌다. 국민들은 마땅한 땔감을 찾게 되었고, 연탄이 나무를 대체하게 되었다. 그 후 대구에서 성공한 것과는 비교할 수 없을 정도로 서울에서 대성공을 거두게 되었다. 나무를 자르면 법을 어기는 것이 되니 사람들이 물밀듯이 밀려와 연탄을 구입해 갔다. 연탄공장이 엄청나게 확장되었고 그 결과 대성그룹은 연탄사업 하나만으로도 당시 국내 10대 그룹에 오르게 되었다.

아울러 연탄사업은 우리 국토의 나무를 잘 보존시켜서 울창하고 푸른 산을 만드는 것에 크게 일조하였다. 이처럼 대성그룹은 항상 공익과 환경을 우선시하는 기업이념을 가지고, 국민 생활의 질을 개선시키고 후손들에게 아름다운 환경을 물려주는 데 최선을 다하고자 노력해 왔다.

3. The Seoul Briquette Factory a Groundbreaking Success

In 1958, when I first arrived in Seoul, there were still many homes that burned firewood. The briquettes we began to produce were a lot more convenient than having to chop wood for a fire. Soon crowds of people began to visit our factory, and briquette sales skyrocketed. After we renovated the briquette factory and just as we were about to open it, President Jung Hee Park declared a new forestation policy prohibiting entrance into all wooded areas. Before the policy was declared, people cut down trees and used the wood for fire in their homes, but now no one had a choice but to look for a new alternative energy source. Soon briquettes replaced wood and began to be used in the homes of Koreans. The success of our briquette factory in Daegu was nothing in comparison to the success of our factory in Seoul. Everyone switched to briquettes, for the cutting down of trees and burning of wood was prohibited by law. As a result of the briquette factory's amazing success and expansion in Seoul, the Daesung Group was ranked among the top ten *jaebeol* (large business conglomerates) in Korea for its success in the briquette business.

The briquette business played a primary role in protecting Korea's trees, which today have grown into rich forest areas. The Daesung Group continues to place top priority on

　이때부터 해외유전, 석탄, 가스전 개발사업에도 눈을 돌리기 시작했다. 전국경제인연합회 회장단과 함께 일본, 미국, 캐나다, 유럽, 동남아, 아프리카 등 세계 여러 나라의 정상들과 기업인들을 찾아 방문하면서 경제적으로 협력할 방안들을 모색하였다. 또한 세계를 향한 도약을 준비하면서 유학 중인 자녀들을 만나 함께 여행하는 것이 나와 네 엄마에게 큰 기쁨이 되었다.

working for the common good and on sustaining the environment, in hopes of enhancing the quality of life of all citizens and leaving our descendants with a beautiful environment.

It was from this time that I turned my eyes and interest towards foreign oil fields, coal, and gas fields. I traveled with members of the Federation of Korean Industries (FKI) all around the world—Japan, the U.S.A., Canada, Europe, Southeast Asia, and Africa—meeting leading experts and businessmen to discuss efforts for economic cooperation. It was your mother's and my great joy to have the chance to visit and travel with you, my children, when you were studying abroad.

4. 돈암장으로 이사하고

당시 내게 큰 숙제는 가족들을 서울로 데리고 오는 것이었다. 7남매가 마음껏 뛰놀 수 있는 마땅한 집을 구하는 것은 쉽지 않았다. 그때 네 엄마가 기도하여 응답으로 받게 된 집이 돈암장이었다. 네 엄마와 나는 매우 감사했다.

우리가 얻게 된 돈암장은 이승만 박사가 귀국하여 대한민국 정부를 수립했던 역사의 산실이었다. 이 집은 창덕궁을 지은 궁중목수의 마지막 후계자 배기한 목수가 1939년 북해도 향나무로 지은 집이었다. 669평이 되는 집의 앞마당에는 큰 잣나무, 벚나무, 향나무가 아름드리 서 있고, 본체는 큰 돌계단 위에 안정감을 가지고 웅장하게 배치되어 있었다. 본체의 마루 천정은 우물정자 모양의 우아한 조각이 들어 있고, 처마는 궁궐과 같이 두 켜로 된 목재 조각이 곡선으로 이어져, 한국건축의 가장 아름다운 표본으로 이름난 곳이다. 특히 안방, 건넌방의 벽에는 동양화가 가득 그려져 있었다. 집을 살 당시에는 잘 몰랐는데 20년 후 조사해 보니, 동양화의 대가들이 그린 것으로 그림마다 값을 매길 수 없는 가치를 가지는 것으로 감정되었다. 네 엄마는 평생 절제운동을 해오면서 그림 한 장 사 모은 적 없이 검소하게 살았는데, 이처럼 귀하고 값진 동양화들을 간직할 수 있게 되었으니 하나님의 신실하신 은혜

4. Living at Don Am Jang

My greatest task at the time was to bring my entire family to Seoul. It wasn't easy for your mother and me to find a house suitable for all seven of you children to run around in. God's answer to your mother's prayers for the provision of a house was Don Am Jang. Your mother and I were grateful.

Don Am Jang was the place that Dr. Syngman Rhee lived in upon returning to Korea from America, and it was also the very place that witnessed the birth of the new government of the Republic of Korea. The house was built in 1939 by a carpenter named Gi Han Bae, who was the last disciple of the school of Won Sik Choi—the royal carpenter who built Changdeok Palace. The house was 669 *pyeong* (2,200 square meters) in area and was built of juniper wood. Beautiful pine trees, cherry trees, and juniper trees grew in the front yard, and the grand house stood at the top of a flight of stone steps.

The ceiling in the living room was covered with wood latticework that made beautiful crisscross patterns. The eaves were like those of a royal palace, with overlapping layers of wood in curved lines. Don Am Jang has gained wide recognition as a prime representative of the beauty of Korean traditional architecture. A special feature of Don Am Jang is the wall in the room across from the master bedroom, which is beautifully decorated with oriental paintings. We had no idea that the paintings had been done by renowned Korean master painters, nor were we aware that each of the paintings

에 감동하지 않을 수 없었다.

네 엄마는 40세가 되었을 때 이 집의 안주인으로 들어왔다. 평생 근검절약하며 많은 길 잃은 영혼들을 돈암장으로 초대하여 마가의 다락방과 같은 귀한 장소로 사용하였다. 돈암장에서 네 엄마의 전도를 받고 하나님의 구원을 깨달아 알고 그리스도를 전하는 삶에 헌신한 사람들도 부지기수로 늘어갔다. 또한 돈암장은 그 자체가 박물관 같아서 네 엄마가 부지런히 잘 관리하여, 오고 가는 많은 외국인 대사들과 세계 유수의 기업 회장단들에게 중요한 외교의 산실이 되기도 하였다.

이 집을 자손대대로 하나님의 영광을 나타내는 은혜의 장소로 잘 보존하길 바란다. 한국 근대사의 궤적을 담고 있는 돈암장이 향후에도 계속 그리스도의 나라를 세우는 집으로 쓰이게 되길 바란다. 그와 함께 한국에서도 우수한 과학자들이 배출되어 노벨상을 받을 수 있도록 해강과학문화재단을 설립하고 잘 지원해주길 당부한다.

was extremely valuable until twenty years later, when we had them appraised. Your mother had lived a humble life, serving the Korea Woman's Temperance Union (KWCTU) and never buying a single work of art. Yet there she lived, in a home adorned with valuable oriental paintings. Her heart could not help but leap in awe of God's goodness and grace.

Your mother became the lady of Don Am Jang at the age of forty. She devoted her lifetime to being a good steward of God's financial blessings and inviting lost souls to Don Am Jang, making the house like Mark's upper room. Through your mother's evangelistic efforts, countless people have come to know about God's saving grace, and they have become faithful servants who themselves share Christ with others. Don Am Jang is a veritable museum, so your mother took special care of the house. She was a diplomat in its truest sense, inviting foreign ambassadors and the world's leading CEOs to our home.

I ask that you, my children, maintain Don Am Jang in good condition so that it may be passed on to future generations as a place where God's grace and glory dwells. I hope that Don Am Jang will continue to be used as a place where God's kingdom may be made manifest for generations to come. I also ask that you, my children, establish and fund a science foundation so that Korea too may nurture scientists and Nobel Prize recipients.

Chapter 4
A God Who is Near in Times of Hardship
위기에 함께 하시는 하나님

대구도시가스 본사 사옥
Daegu City Gas head office

대구도시가스 순시
Round of calls to the city
gas offices (1993)

경북도시가스 창립
Establishment of Gyeongbuk City Gas Co., Ltd. (1997)

김수근 대성그룹 창업회장과 여귀옥 명예회장 금혼식
Our golden wedding anniversary (1991)

여귀옥 명예회장 고희
My wife's 70th birthday (1993)

김영훈 대성그룹 회장 결혼
Younghoon's Wedding (1993)

1. 천연가스 사업 시작

　1973년과 1978년 1차, 2차 오일쇼크를 거친 후 1980년대
에 들어서 세계 에너지환경을 분석하는 가운데, 새로운 미래
에너지는 천연가스가 될 것이라는 결론을 얻었다. 그래서 나
는 1983년 대구도시가스와 서울도시가스를 인수하고 얼마 후
에 경북도시가스를 인수했다. 그 결과 전국 도시가스의 20%
이상을 대성그룹에서 공급할 수 있게 되었다.

　천연가스는 환경친화적인 에너지라는 데 큰 기쁨과 보람이
있었다. 기업은 공익을 추구하며 수익을 남길 때 지속적으로
성공하는 기업으로 나아갈 수 있다. 대성그룹은 에너지사업을
친환경사업으로 확대시켜감으로써 계속하여 성장세를 이어갈
수 있었다.

1. Starting the Natural Gas Business

Following the oil shocks of 1973 and 1978, and entering a new decade, I came to the conclusion that trends in the global energy environment indicated a turn towards natural gas as the energy of the future. In 1983, the Daesung Group acquired Daegu City Gas Co., Ltd., and Seoul City Gas Co., Ltd.; shortly after, we also acquired Gyeongbuk City Gas Co., Ltd. The Group was by then providing natural gas to 20 percent of all of Korea.

Natural gas, as an environmentally friendly energy source, has greatly benefited everyone. When a business operates in dual pursuit of returns and public interest, it can advance, attaining steady success. The Daesung Group has been experiencing continuous growth as an environmentally friendly energy enterprise.

2. 대구 지하철공사 현장 가스 폭발

1995년 봄에 있었던 중요한 사건을 후손들이 잊지 않도록 기록으로 남기고 싶다. 그날 나는 여느 때와 다름없이 아침 8시에 상쾌한 마음으로 출근했다. 사무실에 들어가니 직원들이 TV 앞에 모여 다들 넋을 놓고 있어서 이상한 예감이 들었다. 출근 직후의 회사 모습치곤 심상치 않아서 "왜 아침부터 TV를 보고 있는가?"하고 물었다. 그때 기조실장으로 있던 영훈이가 "아버지, 대구에서 도시 가스가 폭발했습니다."라고 대답했다. TV를 보니 상황이 너무나도 처참했다. 사고현장은 온통 잿더미였고 완전히 전쟁터와 같은 모습이었다. 수많은 사람들이 사망한 것으로 추정했는데, 실제 100여명이 생명을 잃은 대형 사고였다. 나는 "아, 우리 회사는 이제 다 끝났구나." 하고 생각했다. 백여 명이 생명을 잃은 큰 사고에 대한 도의적인 책임을 생각할 때, 배상을 하더라도 실추된 기업이미지를 어떻게 회복시킬 것이며, 가족을 잃은 수많은 시민들의 마음을 어떻게 위로할 수 있단 말인가!

그때 영훈이는 침착한 모습으로 집무실에 들어갔다. 지금까지 우리와 함께하신 하나님께서 이 상황 속에서도 함께 계심을 확실히 믿는 믿음 때문이었다. 큰 사건 한복판에서 공의와 사랑으로 다스리고 계신 하나님에 대한 확고한 믿음으로

2. Daegu Subway Construction Accident

It is my hope that my descendants and the generations to come do not forget the important incident that occurred in spring 1995. I went to work at 8 o'clock in the morning with a refreshed heart, just as I had every other day. When I stepped into the office, all the staff members were gathered around the television, completely absorbed. A strange premonition swept over me. The view of the staff members around the television, especially that early in the morning, was so out of the ordinary that I had to ask them why all of them were so focused on the television. Just then Younghoon, who was working as the head of the Office of Planning and Administration at the time, walked in and said, "Father! Gas lines have exploded in Daegu!" The footage I saw on television was truly horrific. The site of the explosion was covered with ashes; it looked like a battlefield. Reporters announced that many lives had been lost in the accident. The accident was indeed devastating, killing more than 100 people. I thought to myself, *I guess our company has finally reached the end of the road.* When I thought of how the Daesung Group may be morally responsible for the deaths of so many people, I was overwhelmed by the challenge to find ways to restore the company's reputation, and to comfort the families, beyond providing compensation, that had lost their

업무를 시작하는 영훈이를 보면서 나는 큰 힘을 얻었다.

한 시간 정도 지나 대구에서 전화가 왔다면서 영훈이는 내게 참으로 놀라운 보고를 전했다. 폭발 현장의 가스 파이프의 어디도 새는 곳이 없다는 것이었다. 사고 후 경찰은 제일 먼저 폭발 현장의 가스 파이프가 어디에서 새고 있는지 조사해 보았다. 그런데 가스를 집어 넣어 새는 곳을 찾기 위해 아무리 압력을 넣어도 파이프의 결함을 찾을 수가 없었다고 했다. 사고가 난 후 한 시간이 채 되지 않아 현장조사 결과를 발표한 경찰은 이 사건은 대구도시가스의 폭발사고가 아니라고 전했다. 그 조사 결과를 들으면서 나는 말로 표현할 수 없는 하나님의 크신 구원 앞에서 깊이 감사하였다.

loved ones in the incident.

That's when Younghoon, surprisingly calm, entered his office. He knew that the Lord was near, that He had been faithful throughout the years. Younghoon trusted that God would continue to be with us and guide us this time also. I gained great strength in seeing Younghoon start his daily work and duties with an unshakeable faith in God, who was at the center of the scene, governing by His love and providence.

About an hour had passed when Younghoon received a phone call from Daegu and raced into my room to inform me of truly miraculous news. He had been informed that nowhere at the scene of the explosion had anyone found a leaking gas pipe. The police arrived at the scene to carry out investigations. They filled the pipelines with gas from end to end, but no matter how much gas pressure was added, they could not find any leaks. They searched and searched but came to the same conclusion each time. And within an hour's time since the explosion, the police reported that Daegu City Gas Co. was in no way responsible for the Daegu subway construction accident. In hearing those words, I was filled with thanksgiving—thanksgiving that my heart could never contain—for God's deliverance.

3. 가스폭발 사고의 전말

　경찰은 가스관 파열 발생지점을 계속해서 열심히 찾아가다가, 사고 현장에서 200 ~ 300미터 떨어진 지점에서 파손된 가스관을 발견하였다. 그 곳은 모 기업이 확장공사를 하면서 지반을 강화하기 위해 땅에 깊이 구멍을 뚫고 콘크리트로 채워 넣던 작업 현장이었다. 굴착 경험이 없는 사람이 이 일을 맡았던 것이 문제의 발단이었다. 그는 굴착해서는 안 된다는 성고로 박아 놓은 도시가스관 매설 표지판을 무시한 채 계속 뚫고 내려갔다. 그렇게 위험천만한 작업을 진행하다가 결국 도시가스관을 굴착기로 파손시킨 것이다. 곧바로 가스가 분수처럼 흘러나왔다. 그때 신속하게 경찰에 가스관 파손신고를 했더라면 큰 문제가 없었을 것이다. 안타깝게도 이 사람은 가스가 솟아나오자 겁을 먹고 공사현장을 그대로 버려둔 채 도망을 가버렸다. 그 후 몇 시간 동안 유출된 가스는 땅 밑에서 하수관을 따라 지하철 공사 현장으로 흘러가 쌓이게 되었다.

　지하철 공사 현장에는 수천 개의 복공판, 즉 2~3미터 크기의 철판들을 깔아놓는데 그 밑에 도시가스가 흘러 들어가서 여러 시간 동안 계속 가스가 쌓여갔다. 짐작하건대 아침 출근시간에 자동차가 복공판 위로 지나가면서 스파크를 일으켰던 것 같다. 혹은 기사들이 내던진 담배꽁초가 인화를 일으켰을

3. Details of the Gas Explosion

The police searched for a possible leak in the gas pipes until finally, they discovered a damaged gas pipe about 200 to 300 meters away from the scene of the explosion. A company that was constructing a building in the area was digging holes in the ground and filling them up with concrete to make the foundation solid. An individual who was inexperienced at excavation work had been left in charge of the construction. This individual disregarded gas pipeline warning signs and instead decided to dig towards the pipelines. Finally, he pierced through a gas pipeline with the excavator, immediately releasing a fountainlike flow of gas. Even then, if that individual had gone to the police to report a leaking gas pipe, some of the devastating outcomes could have been prevented. Unfortunately, the individual, seeing the gas seep out and in fear for his life, fled from the site. The gas, which was left to leak for hours, made its way through the underground sewer pipes, eventually making its way to the nearby subway construction area.

At the subway construction site nearby, thousands of two- to three-meter steel plates lay fixed to one another to cover deeply dug holes in the ground. It seems the gas that had escaped for hours had settled in the area. It is highly likely that the morning taxis, when passing over the steel plates,

수도 있다. 아무튼 모여있던 가스가 갑자기 발화되어 폭발하면서 폭탄이 터지는 위력의 큰 사고를 일으킨 것이다.

created friction, and thus caused sparks that set off the explosion. Another possibility is that perhaps one of the taxi drivers threw a cigarette butt out onto the steel plates, igniting the gas. Either way, the layers of gas that had settled at the subway construction site were somehow set off, causing a massive explosion like that caused by a bomb.

4. 가스관을 지켜주신 하나님 은혜

2,000~3,000개의 복공판이 하늘로 치솟는 광경을 현장에 있던 사람들이 보니, 폭발 현장의 복공판들이 포물선을 그리면서 산같이 날아 올라 낙엽같이 떨어졌다고 한다. 낙하하는 그 수천 개의 무거운 복공판이 길게 깔려 있던 가스관 위로는 한 개도 떨어지지 않았다는 사실은 도저히 상식적으로 이해하기 힘든 기적이었다. 만약 복공판 중에 한 개라도 가스관 위로 떨어졌다면 엄청난 무게가 주는 충격을 가스관은 버텨낼 수 없었을 것이다. 그렇게 되었다면 경찰이 "이 사고는 분명히 대구도시가스의 가스관 파열로 일어났다."라고 발표했을 것이다. 만약 경찰이 대구도시가스에 사고 책임이 있다고 단정하고 더 이상 수사를 진행하지 않았더라면, 200~300미터 떨어져 있던 모 기업 공사장에 계속 가스가 새어 나와 2차, 3차의 연쇄 폭발이 일어나서 더 큰 인명피해가 났을 것이었다.

하나님께서 대구도시가스의 가스관을 지켜주셔서 더욱 크고 무서운 폭발의 위험을 막아주셨다. 그날 아침 대구도시가스 직원들은 폭발사고 소식을 듣자 즉시 현장에 달려가 가스 밸브를 잠갔다. 대형사고의 위기상황에서 신속하게 대처함으로써 더 큰 폭발사고를 사전에 막을 수 있었다. 이 모든 과정에서 나는 하나님께서 대구도시가스를 지켜주셨음을 볼 수 있었다.

4. God' s Grace and Protection of the Gas Pipes

Eye witnesses described how 2000 to 3000 steel plates shot up in a parabolic projectile path, forming a mountain of heavy steel as they fell to the ground. It is hard to comprehend how not a single one of the thousands of plates that went air-borne had landed on the gas pipelines which extended all across the area. Even if a single steel plate had fallen on a pipeline, the heavy impact of that single plate would have been far too great for the pipeline not to burst. If that had happened, the police would surely have reported that the explosion was the result of leaking pipelines that belonged to Daegu City Gas Co. If the police had concluded that Daegu City Gas Co. was fully responsible for the accident and had decided to stop further investigations, the gas that was leaking 200 to 300 meters away at the construction site would have continued to make its way to the subway construction site, and thereby set off a second and possibly a third explosion, killing many more.

God watched over Daegu gas pipelines and prevented greater, more devastating explosions from occurring. Upon hearing news of the explosion on the morning of the incident, Daegu City Gas Co. employees immediately rushed to the scene to close the gas valves. Despite the aftermath of the large-scale, fatal accident that lay before them, our staff

　　본격적으로 모 기업은 과실에 대한 면밀한 수사를 받게 되
었다. 경찰에서 이것은 모 기업 책임의 건설사고이지 가스사
고가 아니라고 발표했다. 그러자 건설교통부와 산업자원부 사
이의 굉장한 긴장상태가 조성되었다.

members followed all safety procedures and were thus able to prevent a greater explosion from occurring. Through this incident I was able to see God's guiding hand on Daegu City Gas Co. more clearly.

The company doing the construction was subjected to close examination for its errors. The police reported that that company was responsible for the accident, and greater tension began to develop between the Ministry of Construction and Transportation and the Ministry of Commerce, Industry and Energy.

5. 언론의 총공격

　언론은 그때부터 대구도시가스를 감싸주려는 의도로 경찰이 현장조사를 조작하여 발표했다고 보도하기 시작했다. 누가 봐도 그렇게 오해할 소지가 많았다. 대구에서 도시가스가 폭발했는데 대구도시가스는 아무 책임이 없고 모 기업이 전적으로 책임이 있다고 하니까 말이다. 급기야 언론은 대구도시가스를 총공격하기에 이르렀다.

　주요 뉴스에서 "대구도시가스가 폭발해서"라고 발표하면서 모든 책임을 대구도시가스가 져야 하는데 사고의 원인이 잘못 다뤄지고 있다고 분개하며 보도했다. 그때 영훈이가 말했다. "아버지! 하나님께서 불 가운데서 다니엘의 세 친구를 구원하셔서 머리털 하나 타지 않게 지켜 주셨던 것 같이 그 폭발현장에서 우리 가스관을 지켜 주셨습니다. 대구도시가스에 책임이 있다고 공격하면서, 폭발사건을 일으킨 것도 문제가 큰데 경찰과 공모하여 사건을 은폐하고 있다고 지금 모든 언론들이 비방하니, 아버지 마음이 많이 불편하시지요. TV만 틀면 대구도시가스를 비방하니까 신혼에다 첫 아기가 8개월밖에 되지 않은 저도 많이 힘듭니다. 그러나 사자 굴 속에서 다니엘을 지키시기 위해 사자의 입을 막으신 하나님께서 언론이 잘 모르고 보도하는 모든 공격을 곧 잠잠하게 하실 테니 너무

5. Full-Scale Attack by the Media

The media began to report that police had filed false investigation reports in order to protect Daegu City Gas Co. I couldn't blame them; even I could understand how it didn't make any sense that Daegu City Gas Co. was in no way responsible for what appeared to be a gas explosion. The press continued with its full-scale attack on Daegu City Gas Co.

Every time I turned on the television, breaking news reports with headlines such as "DAEGU CITY GAS EXPLODES" claimed that Daegu City Gas Co. was responsible for the explosion but was off the hook because of inaccurate investigation reports. It was then that Younghoon said, "Father! Just as God protected Daniel's three friends from the fire in the blazing furnace, allowing them to remain safe without a single strand of hair harmed, He also protected our gas pipes in the midst of the explosions. I can imagine how distressed your heart is as media reports insist that Daegu City Gas Co. is fully responsible for the gas explosions and even that Daegu City Gas Co. conspired with the police to conceal evidence. Every time I turn on the television, I only hear accusations made against Daegu City Gas Co. I am the young father of an eight-month-old baby boy; I too am struggling. But do not be anxious Father, for God, who closed the mouths of the lions and rescued Daniel from the den of lions,

염려하지 마세요."라고 말했다. 영훈이의 확신에 찬 그 말은 내게 말할 수 없는 큰 평안과 위로를 주었다. 신문에서는 연일 대문짝만한 토픽 뉴스로 대구도시가스가 폭발사고의 주범이라고 나오고, 저녁마다 TV주요 뉴스에서 대구도시가스를 공격하였다. 하지만 침착하게 과정을 주시하는 영훈이의 든든한 모습이 곁에 있어서 많은 격려가 되었다.

그때 사고에 대한 증인으로 대구시의 한 환경미화원이 나타났다. 그는 신문기자들 앞에서 "사고 당일 건설현장이었던 지하철 공사장을 지나다가 가스 새는 냄새를 맡았다."고 증언했다. 기자들은 마치 특종을 잡은 것처럼 그 사람의 얼굴을 신문에 크게 실었다. 드디어 대구도시가스의 안전관리 문제로 폭발했다는 단서를 찾았다고 하면서 대서특필한 것이다. 다음 날 같은 사람이 "나는 냄새를 못 맡았다."고 정반대로 증언했다. 그러자 기자들은 경찰이 환경미화원을 협박해서 증언을 번복하도록 했다며 더욱 불리한 상황으로 우리를 몰아갔다.

그 환경미화원이 몇 번을 엎치락뒤치락 말을 바꾼 후 그의 장모가 나타나 기자들에게 말했다. "이 사람의 말을 절대로 믿지 마세요. 이 사람은 평소에 거짓말을 많이 하는 사람이니까 절대로 믿어서는 안 됩니다."라고. 그 후로 기자들은 갑자기 맥이 쑥 빠지게 되었다. 더 이상은 추측기사를 쓰지 못하게 된

will also silence the false accusations of the media in His time. So do not fret, Father."

Younghoon's words of conviction encouraged me and gave me great strength and peace. In large, bold print, newspaper headlines deemed Daegu City Gas Co. responsible for the explosion; and the news channels in the evening weren't an exception as they too attacked Daegu City Gas Co. But I was deeply encouraged in having Younghoon, calm and in control, by my side.

A Daegu sanitation worker stepped up to testify as a witness to the incident. He proclaimed before a crowd of journalists, "On the day of the explosion, I was walking by the subway construction site and I could smell gas." The journalists, as though they had found exclusive, breaking news, had the man's picture printed in newspapers. It seemed the newspaper headlines were a step closer to proving that the incident had occurred because of Daegu City Gas Co.'s failure to follow safety precautions. The next day, that same man spoke again and said that he had *not* smelled gas in the area. In seeing this man take back his words, the journalists believed the police to have threatened the sanitation worker to change his testimony.

The sanitation worker continued to go back and forth between his testimonies, until finally his mother-in-law appeared before the journalists and said, "Do not believe a

것이다. 그들은 그 환경미화원을 TV 카메라 앞에 세우고, "이제 정말 바른대로 진술하라."고 추궁하니까, 그는 TV에 나와 주목 받고 싶어서 이제까지 거짓말을 했다고 실토했다. 기자들은 너무 어이가 없어서 아예 입을 다물어버렸다. 사자같이 공격하며 추측 보도를 내보내던 언론의 입도 그만 닫히게 되었다.

그 후 모 기업과 대구도시가스 사이에서 큰 재판이 있었다. 경찰이 모 기업에게 사고에 대한 책임 배상을 하라고 하니까, 모 기업은 그때까지도 대구도시가스 책임이라고 주장하면서 재판을 대법원까지 끌고 갔다. 결국 대법원에서도 대구도시가스는 아무 책임이 없는 것으로 최종 판결이 나왔다. 판결에 따라 모 기업이 500억 원을 배상했고, 대구도시가스는 큰 슬픔과 고통 중에 있는 분들을 위로하는 뜻으로 성금을 내어 사고 수습에 최선을 다했다. 가족을 불시에 잃은 수많은 가정들이 겪게 된 그 엄청난 슬픔을 누가 다 헤아려 위로할 수 있겠는가! 대구도시가스 임직원들과 나는 큰 상처를 입은 분들에게 조금이나마 위로가 되고자 노력했다. 아무리 위로해도 충분히 위로할 길이 없던 이 엄청난 사고를 겪으면서, 놀라우신 하나님의 구원과 은혜를 동시에 경험하였다. 이 후로 도시가스사업을 진행하면서 안전사고를 예방하는 데 최우선 순위를 두어

word this man says. This man is a liar. Do not believe what he says." In hearing this woman speak against her son-in-law, the journalists turned away in disappointment. They were no longer permitted to write speculative news articles regarding this incident, so they confronted the sanitation worker on national television: "This is your last chance to tell the truth." Smiling, the man confessed that he had made false testimonies in order to gain attention and appear on television. The journalists were so dumbfounded that they remained speechless, and finally, the lionlike attacks and speculations ceased, and the mouths of the media were sealed shut.

Shortly after this, Daegu City Gas Co. and the company that was doing the construction work went to court. When the police attested to the company's responsibility for the gas explosions and ordered them to pay compensation, the company continued to claim that Daegu City Gas Co. was responsible. They eventually took the case to the Supreme Court. In the end, however, the Supreme Court found Daegu City Gas Co. clear of all responsibility, and the other company was ordered to pay compensation in the amount of 50 billion won. In the hopes of comforting and consoling those who lost their loved ones in the accident, Daegu City Gas Co. did all it could through financial support to help clean up the city. Who could ever fully understand the pain and sorrow the families of those killed in the accident

왔다. 항상 당부해왔듯이 우리 도시가스사업은 청정연료인 도
시가스만을 공급하는 것이 아니라 안전도 함께 서비스하는 사
업이라는 것을 깊이 명심해주기를 바란다.

experienced? The staff at Daegu City Gas Co. and I humbly made efforts to comfort them. In enduring this devastating incident, in which no form of comfort but God's could ever come close to being sufficient, I experienced God's truly amazing grace. Ever since the incident, the Daesung Group has placed priority on safety precautions. As I have always told you my children, keep in mind that we provide not only clean gas but also safety.

6. 믿음이 주는 담대함

　가장 큰 위기에서 가장 큰 구원을 경험한 이 이야기를 후손들에게 전해주길 바란다. 지금 세상에는 악이 가득하다. 하나님의 말씀을 모르면 이 악에 우리가 중독되어 버린다. 그러나 말씀을 굳게 믿으면 우리는 선한 싸움을 싸울 수 있게 된다. 하나님의 도우심으로 악과 싸워서 이길 수 있게 되는 것이다. 성경 말씀에 "악에게 지지 말고, 선으로 악을 이기라."고 말씀하셨다(로마서 12:21). 찬송가에도 "선한 싸움 다 싸우고 의의 면류관 받아쓰리라."는 가사가 있다(찬송가 402장). 이번 일만 해도 언론의 공격으로 우리가 크게 요동했다면 폭풍 속에서 파산하는 배처럼 되고 말았을 것이다. 그러나 영훈이가 시종 침착하게 방향타를 잡고 큰 파도를 이기고 현명하게 대처한 것이 내게 큰 힘이 되었다. 이 폭발사건은 매우 큰 사고여서 온 세계에 토픽뉴스로 보도되었다. 이 사건의 핵심을 아는 사람은 영훈이밖에 없다고 생각한다. 그 사고의 중심에서 더 큰 사고를 막아주신 하나님의 은혜를 누구보다도 깊이 경험하고 깨달았기 때문이다. 수천 개의 복공판이 날아서 낙엽같이 떨어질 때 하나님께서 대구도시가스와 대성그룹을 지켜주셨다. 나는 그 이유를 이 땅에 하나님의 나라를 세우는 데 대성그룹이 맡을 책임이 있기 때문이라고 생각한다. 하나님께서

6. Courage in Faith

I hope this story about the amazing grace I experienced during my greatest trial may reach generations to come. The world is filled with evil and wickedness. If we do not know God's Word, we become vulnerable to that which is evil, but if we put our wholehearted faith in His Word, we are equipped to fight the good fight of faith. Through God's guidance and protection, we will claim victory in our fight against evil, for it is written: *"Do not be overcome by evil, but overcome evil with good" (Romans 12:21)*; and also in Hymn 402: *"And when the battle's over we shall wear a crown."* If we had rocked the boat from side to side when the media attacked Daegu City Gas Co., we would not have survived the violent storms that struck us and our boat would have been destroyed. Younghoon calmly placed his hands on the rudder and wisely steered us through the huge waves. The Daegu subway construction accident was so big that it was reported worldwide. I believe Younghoon was the only one who did not lose focus or forget who was at the center throughout it all. Younghoon recognized all along that God stood at the center of the entire incident and, because of His grace, shielded us from greater disaster. When the thousands of steel plates flew through the air and fell to the ground, God was at the center, protecting Daegu City Gas Co. and the

큰 사랑으로 우리를 구원해 주셨음을 깨달을수록 우리는 더욱 겸손해져야 한다. 우리를 구원하신 하나님의 은혜에 감사하면서 주어진 사명을 잘 감당할 수 있도록 더욱 더 분발하여라.

Daesung Group. I believe God showed His amazing grace because He wanted to use the Daesung Group to build His kingdom on earth. The more we realize the depth of His grace, the more we must humble our hearts. Continue, my children, to live with thanksgiving for God's grace and to carry out the Great Commission.

7. 금혼식, 고희, 그리고 영훈이의 결혼

  1991년 11월에는 가정적으로 매우 큰 복을 받았다. 아들 하나만 낳아도 성공이라 할 수 있는 폐결핵에 걸려 소망이 거의 없는 결혼생활을 시작했던 나와 네 엄마가 결혼 50주년을 기념하는 금혼식을 맞이하게 된 것이다. 일가친척들이 모두 축하하는 그 자리에 섰을 때, 나는 참으로 믿기지 않았다. 나의 많은 부족함에도 불구하고 하나님께서 귀한 가정을 이룰 수 있게 해주시고 50년을 한결같은 은혜로 지켜 주신 것에 대해 그 무엇으로 감사드려야 할지 가늠조차 할 수 없었다. 자녀와 손자 손녀들의 재롱을 보면서 맞이한 금혼식은 하나님의 신실하신 사랑과 축복의 증거였다.

  1993년에는 또 네 엄마가 고희를 맞이하게 되어 기쁨으로 온 가족들이 함께 모여 축하할 수 있었다. 그때 우리 가정에 한 가지 소원이 있었는데 바로 영훈이가 결혼하는 것이었다.

  이 소원은 바로 얼마 후 그 해에 이루어졌다. 네 엄마와 온 가족들이 함께 기도해오던 대로 믿음의 가정에서 자란 현숙한 여인을 만나 영훈이가 가정을 이루게 되었다. 나와 네 엄마와 모든 가족들은 매우 기뻐했다. 영훈이가 첫아들을 안고 돈암

7. Our Golden Wedding Anniversary, a 70th Birthday Celebration, and Younghoon's Wedding

Your mother had married me, a man suffering from tuberculosis and predicted surely to die, in spite of being told that it would take a miracle for me to live long enough for her to give birth to a son. In 1991, your mother and I were blessed with the occasion of celebrating our golden wedding anniversary. I could hardly believe that I was actually surrounded by all our relatives who had gathered to bless your mother and me on this special occasion. Despite my many weaknesses, God blessed me with a wonderful family. For fifty years God, with his unchanging grace, has been my protection. His infinite blessings leave me absolutely still and silent, unable to even begin to say how grateful I am. The very fact that I was able to celebrate my golden wedding anniversary with my children and grandchildren is a testimony in itself to God's unchanging love and overflowing blessings.

In 1993, we all gathered again with joyful hearts to celebrate your mother's 70th birthday and to wish her continued health and happiness. The one wish our family had, though, was that Younghoon get married.

This wish of ours came true later that year. Just as your mother and the entire family had prayed for years, God had prepared a wise and virtuous wife who had been raised in a family of faith for Younghoon. Your mother and I, as well as

장에 올 때면 나는 잘 간직해 둔 과자를 손자와 나누어 먹으면서 즐거워하곤 하였다.

all of you, my children, were utterly joyous when the two married. I am reminded of how, whenever they brought their firstborn son to Don Am Jang, I took great joy in sharing with him all the cookies and crackers I had kept to the side for him.

Chapter 5
The 1997 East Asian
Financial Crisis in Retrospect
IMF외환
위기회고

대성그룹 창립 50주년
The 50th Anniversary
of the Daesung Group
(May 10, 1997)

대성그룹 관훈동 사옥 매입
The Daesung Group's office building in Gwanhun-dong (1996)

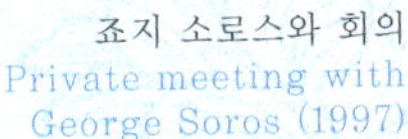

죠지 소로스와 회의
Private meeting with George Soros (1997)

영주천연가스기지 준공
Completion of the natural gas plant in Yeongju (2002)

1. Matching Fund 제안

오늘은 내가 영훈이를 칭찬하는 말을 남기고 싶구나.

1997년 IMF와 같은 절체절명의 금융위기 가운데 대성그룹은 전혀 흔들리지 않으니 모두들 놀라워했다. 다른 회사들과 비교해 볼 때 우리의 채무가 현저하게 낮은 데 대해 많은 이들이 부러운 시선으로 보았다. 한마디로 빚을 멀리한 것이 IMF를 이긴 비결이었다. 영훈이는 "피차 사랑의 빚 외에는 아무에게든지 아무 빚도 지지 말라. (로마서 13:8)"는 성경 말씀을 기업이 추구해야 할 기본 자세로 삼고 실천에 옮겼다.

영훈이가 재무팀을 맡아서 회사 재정을 완전히 새롭게 개선시킨 일은 IMF의 거친 파도 속에서 대성그룹을 순항시킨 가장 큰 이유가 되었다. 특히 미국에서 유학을 마치고 돌아온 영훈이가 회사에서 시행했던 '매칭펀드'는 우리 회사뿐 아니라 한국 금융계에 새로운 사업 모델이 되었다.

에너지 기업인 대성그룹은 겨울에는 자금력이 커서 500억 원 이상의 여유자금을 늘 보유하고 있었다. 그러나 상대적으로 에너지 수요가 적은 여름에는 자금이 부족하여 은행에서 500억 원을 빌려야만 했다. 겨울에는 은행들이 개미떼 같이 모여들어 회사 자금을 유입하고 싶어하면서도 이자는 1퍼센트에서 2퍼센트 범위에 머물러 있었다. 당시 재무팀은 우리가

1. Proposal for Matching Funds

And now I would like to write a few words in praise of Younghoon. Everyone was amazed with how the Daesung Group remained unshaken in the midst of the 1997 East Asian financial crisis. Envious eyes looked to the Group because we were in a comparatively safe position in terms of finance. I believe the secret to our victory in the crisis was our abhorrence of debts. Younghoon, applying the Scripture to his daily life, was especially careful to keep debt at a distance. For it is written: *"Let no debt remain outstanding, except the continuing debt to love one another, for he who loves his fellow man has fulfilled the law." (Romans 13:8)*

The Daesung Group was able to stand firm and cruise over the devastating effects of the financial crisis because Younghoon had managed the company's financial affairs and had reformed the company's financial framework. When Younghoon returned from his studies in the U.S., he proposed the concept of matching funds, which not only changed the Group's financial framework but also introduced the community of Korean banks and financial institutions to a new financial model.

As an energy enterprise, the Daesung Group enjoys excess funds of over 50 billion won during the winter. On the other hand, with summer comes a decrease in demand for energy

은행에 많은 이자를 요구하게 되면 여름에 자금을 빌리기 힘들다는 이유로 낮은 이자로 은행에 돈을 빌려주고 있었다. 그것도 하루 이틀씩 극(極)초 단기자금으로 빌려주는 경우도 있었다. 은행 입장에서는 그래야만 이자 손실을 줄이게 되니 말이다. 반면 여름에 회사는 은행에서 20퍼센트 또는 30퍼센트의 이자를 지불하고 자금을 빌려오고 있었다. 에너지 회사에는 여름에 여유 자금이 없기 때문에 우리는 울며 겨자 먹기 식으로 빌릴 수밖에 없는 것이 당시 관행이었다.

영훈이는 이 관행의 모순성을 지적했다. 동절기 회사에 돈이 많을 때는 1퍼센트, 2퍼센트의 이자만으로 거의 뺏기다시피 자금을 빌려 주고, 여름에는 그 10배 이상의 이자를 내고 은행으로부터 자금을 빌려 오는 것을 모두 중지시켰다. 그리고 시중 은행의 담당자들을 다 불러 모았다. 그들에게 동절기에 우리 회사의 돈이 필요하거든 10퍼센트 정기예금으로 6개월 동안 빌려 주는 새로운 방안을 제안했다. 하루 이틀 빌려가는 대신 10퍼센트를 내서 차입해 가고, 여름에 은행에서 회사로 빌려줄 때는 10.5 퍼센트 정도의 이자로 주도록 한 것이다. 10퍼센트에 빌려주고 10.5퍼센트에 빌리니까 은행은 0.5퍼센트의 이익을 얻게 된다. 이러한 영훈이의 제안에 은행 측에선 모두 동의하였고, 영훈이는 처음으로 '매칭펀드' 란 것을 만들

and a lack of funds of over 50 billion won. In the summer, the Group takes out bank loans. In winter, banks would march like colonies of ants to add our excess funds of over 50 billion won to their inflow at a fixed interest rate of 1 to 2 percent. The Group's Finance Division continued to lend money to banks at a low interest rate for fear that a higher interest rate would make the Group's position vulnerable in the summer when we had to borrow from the banks. On top of that, there were times when we gave out one- or two-day short-term loans, which made it possible for the banks to reduce interest fees. In summer, however, we would take out bank loans at an interest rate of 20 to 30 percent. Since we lacked funds in the summer, we had to bite the bullet and borrow bank loans at high interest rates.

Younghoon pointed out the need to reevaluate the situation. He brought a stop to the cycle of having to lend out money at low interest rates in the winter, only to pay ten times the interest rate to borrow money from banks in the summer. He called for a meeting with all the bank directors in the city. At the meeting Younghoon proposed to give six-month loans to the banks in the winter season at a fixed interest rate of 10 percent. And he informed the bankers that they would be required to pay a 10-percent interest before taking out short-term loans. In return, Younghoon also proposed that the Daesung Group would take bank loans at a

었다. 당시에 그러한 금융상품은 우리나라에는 운용되고 있지 않았다. 나는 이러한 영훈이의 자금운영방식을 무척 새롭고 탁월하게 생각했다. 겨울에 우리에게 자금을 빌려간 은행은 반드시 여름에 같은 금액으로 거래해야 한다는 계약을 성사시킨 것이다.

국내외 은행들이 모두 좋은 제안으로 받아들인 후, 막상 실행에 옮기는 데 있어서는 외국계 은행들이 더 창의적이고 적극적이었다. 우리나라 은행들은 처음에 주춤거리며 거부하려는 움직임이 있었다. 그래서 씨티뱅크, 체이스맨하탄 등 큰 외국계 은행들이 우리 자금 500억 원을 겨울에 빌려 가고 여름에 다시 500억 원을 내주었다. 영훈이가 재무팀을 맡은 2~3년 후에 정산해보니 매년 거의 10퍼센트의 순이익이 우리에게 돌아왔다. 겨울에 500억 원의 10퍼센트가 6개월이면 25억 원의 순익이 되었다. 그 다음 여름에는 또 500억 원을 20퍼센트, 30퍼센트에 빌리던 것을 10퍼센트 정도에 빌리니까 10~20퍼센트의 순익이 계속 남았다. 재무팀의 매칭펀드 운용만으로 대성그룹이 벌어들이는 연간 순익이 매년 50억 원 이상 크게 늘어나게 되었다.

이 일로 나는 그룹의 운영 일체를 안심하고 영훈이에게 일임할 수 있었고, 곧이어 닥친 외환위기는 오히려 우리 대성그

10.5-percent interest rate in the summer. His proposal to lend money at 10 percent and borrow at 10.5 percent ensured the banks a gain of 0.5 percent. The banks accepted Younghoon's proposal and, for the first time, the concept of matching funds was incorporated in the Korean business world. I thought his ideas and suggestions were absolutely brilliant and innovative. In addition, Younghoon also formed an agreement with the banks ensuring that they would give loans to us in the summer at interest rates equal to those applied when they borrowed from us in the winter.

The foreign banks in Korea all accepted the concept of matching funds as a new positive financial model. The national banks of Korea showed much hesitation and seemed to lack interest in the idea, but the foreign banks in Korea were quite enthusiastic about the whole concept. The Daesung Group established matching funds with several large foreign banks, including Citibank and Chase Manhattan Bank, and thus lends out 50 billion won in the winter and is guaranteed the same amount in the summer. Two to three years after Younghoon first became manager of the Finance Division of the Daesung Group, I calculated a 10-percent increase in annual gains, accredited to Younghoon's contributions. Lending out 50 billion won for six months at an interest rate of 10 percent left us with a gain of 2.5 billion won in the winter; and borrowing 50 billion won at an

룹의 건실함을 대내외에 크게 알릴 수 있는 천재일우의 호기
가 되었다.

interest rate of 10.5 percent in the summer, as opposed to the previous 20- to 30-percent interest rate, reduced our costs, leaving us between 10 and 20 percent more of what we had previously paid in interest. Using this system of matching funds alone generates an annual gain that surpasses 5 billion won for the Daesung Group.

Seeing the great success of Younghoon's contributions, I was able to transfer all management authority to him with peace of mind. The financial crisis struck immediately afterwards, but contrary to the conditions the crisis forced others to face, it presented the Daesung Group with a golden opportunity to prove to the world that it was a stable, reputable, reliable enterprise.

2. 관훈동 사옥 입찰

영훈이는 에너지사업이 계절에 따라 자금유동의 변화가 심한 것을 보고, 여름에 자금을 충분히 원활하게 마련할 수 있는 사업으로 건설사업을 제안했다. 건설사업은 우리 그룹이 사옥을 구입한 것을 계기로 곧 활성화되었다.

IMF를 한 해 앞두었던 1996년은 대성그룹 창립 49주년을 축하하는 뜻 깊은 해였다. 그때까지 빚 없는 기업경영과 부동산 투기를 하지 않는다는 원칙을 지켜온 결과로 모든 계열사 사무실들은 세를 지불하고 빌려 쓰고 있었다.

어느 날 네 엄마가 신문 한 귀퉁이에 조그맣게 나온 신한국당 당사 매각 공고 기사를 보았다. 시내 한복판의 큰 부지가 매물로 나오는 것은 흔한 일이 아니었다. 평소 부동산에 전혀 관심이 없던 네 엄마는 그룹 사옥을 마련할 좋은 터가 되겠다고 하며 내게 적극 추천했다.

당시 계열사 사무실들이 흩어져 있어서 결제 시간과 절차에 있어 여간 불편하지 않았다. 사옥 마련의 필요성을 느끼고 있던 차에 영훈이는 그 제안을 기꺼이 실행에 옮겨 입찰에 임하도록 준비하였다. 신한국당 당사에서 세 대통령이 나왔으니 풍수지리설로 용이 나오는 자리라고 하여, 우리의 경쟁사로 나온 S그룹은 두 계열사를 앞세워서 입찰에 적극 참여했다.

2. Bid for the Gwanhun-dong Building

Observing how changes in capital flow varied significantly with the change of seasons, Younghoon suggested that we start a construction business, which he believed would help increase the inflow of capital in the summer. We acquired a building, and soon our construction business was on its way.

The year 1996, just one year before the financial crisis struck East Asia, was a significant year for the Daesung Group as it celebrated its 49th anniversary. Until that time, we did not own an office building. Because of my strong desire to operate a debt-free business and my lack of interest in real-estate investments, our affiliated offices leased office space.

One day, your mother discovered an ad written in small print in the corner of the classified ads section of a newspaper for a building owned by the New Korea Party. Seldom did large buildings, let alone those located in the heart of the city, come up for sale. Your mother had never been interested in real estate, but she suddenly claimed to have found the perfect building for the Daesung Group.

I too had considered looking for an office building, for having all our departments and divisions scattered about in different offices was proving to be highly inconvenient and inefficient. Younghoon took the lead in proceeding with the process of purchasing the office building. Because three presidents had been elected from parties which had occupied

영훈이는 시세에 맞는 정당한 가격을 적어 넣었는데 입찰 결과 바로 지금의 인사동 대성그룹 본사 건물을 인수하게 되었다. 국제 금융을 공부한 영훈이의 아이디어로 단자를 없애고 Matching Fund를 만들어 창출한 여유 자금과 유상 증자를 통해 구입한 사옥에서 IMF를 무사히 지나게 되어 나는 얼마나 기뻤는지 모른다. 그것은 마치 노아의 방주를 타고 안전하게 대홍수를 지나는 것과 같은 은혜였다. 회사의 모든 일을 맡기고 간섭하지 않았던 그 시기에 영훈이는 시종일관 친절한 미소를 지으며 안정적으로 회사를 이끌어주었다.

대성그룹에게 절체절명의 위기가 천재일우의 기회가 될 수 있었던 것은 전적으로 하나님의 은혜였다. 위기를 미리 대처할 수 있게 하신 하나님, 위기를 성장의 기회로 삼게 하신 하나님께 아무리 감사를 드려도 부족하다고 생각한다. 우리가 받은 은혜 위에 은혜를 늘 기억하고 땅끝까지 전하도록 하여라.

that very same building, people deemed the ground where the building stood divine and claimed that mighty dragons were sure to rise from the location. Thus another conglomerate, the 'S Group' , competed against the Daesung Group in the bid for the building.

Younghoon placed a reasonable bid on the building, and the bid was accepted, placing the building in the ownership of the Daesung Group. That building is located in Insa-dong and is where the Group's headquarters is still housed today. Owing to Younghoon's educational background in international finance and the introduction of the concept of matching funds, the Group was able to collect sufficient funds to purchase the building and survive the financial crisis unscathed. I was extremely pleased with the results. It reminded me of the way God's grace protected Noah's ark from the flood. From the beginning when I granted Younghoon full responsibility over the company, he went about his duties and led the company conscientiously and with a friendly smile.

It was entirely God's amazing grace that transformed what could have been the Daesung Group's most tragic experience into a golden opportunity to advance. No matter how many times I utter my thanksgiving to the Lord God almighty, who provided the way for us to steer away from destruction and allowed us to grow in a time of emergency, it will not be adequate. My dear children, never forget the grace upon grace we've been shown and witness to it to the ends of the earth.

3. 단기 부채 상환

　IMF 직전에 몇 년 동안 우리나라 경제는 극도로 불안했다. 그러더니 1997년 말 갑자기 한국 경제가 무너져 내렸다. 우리나라가 국가적으로 부도가 나버린 것이다. 그 전에 영훈이는 10년간 대성그룹 재무팀을 이끌며 경제가 부실해지고 있다고 여러 차례 경고하였다. 나라 경제가 쓰러질지라도 대성그룹은 노아의 방주같이 순항할 수 있도록 재무상태를 치밀하고 단단하게 개선해갔다. 영훈이가 재무팀을 맡은 후 가장 주목했던 것은 단기자금 위주로 돌아가는 당시 재무환경의 불합리한 구조였다. IMF가 닥쳐온 주요 원인 중 하나는 당시 기업들이 단기자금을 쉽게 생각하여 많이 빌려 쓴 것에 있었다. 그러한 위험성으로부터 사전에 조치를 취하고자 IMF가 일어나기 훨씬 전부터 영훈이는 우리 회사의 단기자금을 모두 정리해갔다.

　나는 평생 빚을 싫어해서 영훈이의 그러한 재무 개선 의지를 매우 긍정적으로 보고 적극 지원하였다. 당시 기업들이 쓰던 빚은 3년이나 5년짜리 장기부채가 아니라, 주로 3개월이나 6개월 혹은 길어야 1년이 안 되는 단기부채를 쓰고 있었다. 누가 보아도 당시 기업들의 재무구조는 너무나 취약했다. 영훈이는 우리 회사의 단기부채를 상환하여서 대성그룹은 실질적으로 빚이 거의 없는 회사가 되었다. 그 후 6개월이 채 되지

3. Clearing All Short-term Liabilities

For several years preceding the financial crisis, the Korean economy had not been stable, and in 1997 it crashed to the ground. The entire nation went bankrupt. For a decade prior to the crisis, Younghoon had warned us of how the Korean economy was weakening. He kept a close eye on the Group's financial state and activities. He was determined to strengthen its foundations and prepared to ride through the coming flood like Noah's ark. From the time Younghoon was placed in charge of the Finance Division, he recognized the danger of the overall trend in the local financial environment towards increased short-term loans and debts. One of the key factors that led to the crisis in Korea is said to be the rapid increase in short-term loans and debts. When he detected the possibility of a crisis, Younghoon directed his efforts to clear the Group's short-term debts far before the crisis struck the region.

I had always been one to shun debt, so I fully supported his decision to clear our Group of all its short-term loans and debts. During the time leading up to the crisis, many businesses were taking out three- to six-month short-term loans, as opposed to long-term loans over a period of three to five years. Anyone could see that the situation of Korean businesses was extremely grave. Younghoon cleared all of the Daesung Group's short-term debts, leaving the Group nearly

않아 나라 경제가 무너져 국가적으로 큰 충격에 휩싸이게 되었다. 그 누구도 한국 경제가 그렇게 총체적으로 부도가 날 것이라고는 예상치 못했다. 나는 영훈이의 선견지명과 혜안에 아비로서 매우 든든하였고, 회사의 실무를 일임한 후로 한 번도 후회한 적이 없었다.

debt-free. Just six months later, the financial crisis struck, devastating the Korean economy. Not one single person had known, let alone even imagined, that the entire economy would crash so suddenly without much notice. As his father, I stand amazed, captured by Younghoon's gift of foresight and wise counsel. Never once have I regretted placing the company under Younghoon's leadership.

4. 왜 외환 위기가 일어났던가?

IMF 직전에 태국에 굉장한 건설 붐이 있었다. 그때 우리나라는 신용이 매우 좋은 편이었다. 시중 은행들은 해외에서 적당한 이자로 자본을 들여와 태국에 높은 이자로 빌려주는 식으로 국제금융업을 전개했었다. 태국 기업들은 건설산업에 투자하기 위해 우리나라로부터 돈을 많이 빌려 갔는데, 갑자기 태국 경제가 무너져버렸다. 그 결과 우리나라 경제도 같이 무너지게 된 것이다.

우리가 우리 자본을 빌려 주었으면 큰 타격이 없었을 것이다. 그러나 빌린 돈을 다시 빌려 주었기 때문에 태국이 무너지자 한국 금융기관은 원금을 상환할 능력을 상실하게 되었다. 한국 금융기관들은 태국에 대출해 준 자본을 찾을 수가 없어 도미노 현상으로 밀리면서 같이 무너지고 말았다. 많은 국내 기업들은 금융기관의 단기자금 부채상환 압력에 휘말려 이같이 무너진 것이다.

4. What Led to the Financial Crisis?

Prior to the financial crisis, there was an extreme boom in the construction industry in Thailand. Since Korea maintained good credit standing, Korean banks borrowed foreign loans at a reasonable interest rate, only to lend out loans to Thailand at a high interest rate. Thai construction businesses borrowed mass loans from Korea to invest in the booming Thai construction industry. But when the Thai economy suddenly collapsed, the Korean economy collapsed with it.

Had Korea lent unborrowed money to Thai businesses, Korea would not have suffered such extensive consequences, but because Korea had lent money that it had itself borrowed, when the Thai economy crumbled, the Korean economy suffered also because Korean banks and financial institutions had no means to repay their foreign lenders. In other words, Korean banks and financial institutions could not round up enough money to pay off their foreign loans, and thus the Korean economy fell victim to the domino effect. Numerous Korean companies got entangled in the mess of banks and financial institutions that were struggling with debt repayments, and they too collapsed.

5. IMF 무풍지대

　누구도 예측하지 못했던 급속한 국가부도를 영훈이는 정확하게 예측하였고 빈틈없이 대비하였다. 그 어떤 극한 상황이 와도 흔들리지 않도록 기업의 모든 재무상태를 튼튼하게 개선시켰다. IMF가 터지고 한 달 정도 후에 능률협회에서 전화가 왔다. "회장님, 대성그룹이 지금 재계 10위가 됐습니다."

　대성은 예전에 연탄사업 하나만 가지고도 재계 10위에 올라 있었다. 그 후에 큰 부채를 지지 않고 안정성 위주로 사업을 진행시키면서 50위 정도에 머무르고 있었다. IMF때 많은 기업들이 문을 닫게 되자 대성그룹은 다시 재계 10위로 올라가게 되었다. 신문에서는 IMF 무풍지대 삼총사로 대성그룹, 태광산업, 롯데그룹을 조명하면서 세 그룹의 재무구조가 제일 튼튼하다고 크게 보도하였다. 주요 신문들이 'IMF 무풍지대', 'IMF 삼총사' 라는 제목의 기사로 대성그룹을 다루면서 흔들리지 않는 기업의 벤치마킹 대상으로 우리를 칭찬했던 것을 감사하게 기억하고 있다.

5. The Financial Crisis and the Region of Calm

Younghoon was able to predict the coming of a national financial crisis and thus prepared in advance. He established a new financial framework for the Daesung Group that allowed it to remain stable and secure in a time of crisis. About a month following the onset of the financial crisis, I received a call from the Korea Management Association: "Chairman, the Daesung Group has been listed among the top ten businesses in Korea."

Years before, the Daesung Group's briquette business had been named among the top ten businesses in Korea and, mainly thanks to its relatively debt-free state and safe management, the Group had remained on the list of the top fifty Korean businesses. During the financial crisis, countless businesses filed for bankruptcy and closed, but the Daesung Group was able to rise again to the rank of top ten businesses in Korea. Newspapers named the Daesung Group, Taekwang Industrial Co., and the Lotte Group the "three regions of calm" in the midst of the crisis. It was reported that these three were the most stable groups that remained in good financial standing. The Daesung Group received much praise from journalists and newspapers as a top benchmarking company.

6. 죠지 소로스의 제안

IMF직후에 있었던 일이다. 죠지 소로스라는 해지펀드 전문가가 찾아왔다. 그는 전 세계에서 주식거래를 통해 엄청나게 큰 돈을 번 사람이었다. 국제적으로 주가가 떨어지면 사두었다가 주가가 오르면 파는 방식으로 항상 주식시장의 움직임을 예의주시하며 막대한 수입을 올리고 있었다. 김대중 대통령이 우리나라 경제가 너무 어려우니까 죠지 소로스에게 전화를 했다. 그때 죠지 소로스는 휴가를 떠나 멀리 바하마 해변에서 수영을 즐기고 있었는데, 코리아라는 나라의 대통령으로부터 전화가 왔다고 하니 직접 전화를 받았다. 내용인즉 한국에 와서 도와달라는 부탁을 대통령이 친히 전한 것이었다.

한국에 온 죠지 소로스는 거의 모든 기업들이 무너지고 같이 일할 곳이 없어서 난색을 표하였다. 그는 국내 기업 현황을 면밀히 검토한 끝에 대성그룹을 견실한 기업으로 분석하고 우리를 찾아왔다. 그때 조선호텔에 마련된 회의 석상에서 영훈이는 막내 성주와 함께 동석했다. 죠지 소로스는 우리와 사업을 같이 하자며 몇 가지 제안을 해왔다. 우리나라의 모 은행을 같이 인수하자고 했고, S 증권회사를 인수하여 같이 운영하자는 내용도 덧붙였다. 나는 죠지 소로스의 투자 방식에 대해 쉽게 긍정할 수 없는 부분이 있었다. 죠지 소로스는 국가나 기

6. George Soros' Proposal

Immediately following the onset of the crisis, the expert financial speculator and stock investor George Soros paid us a visit. Soros had accumulated great wealth through investments worldwide. As an expert financial speculator, he kept close observation of trends and changes in the stock market, buying when stock prices fall and selling when they rise. Because the Korean economy was doing so poorly, then-President Kim Dae Jung made a telephone call to Soros. Soros was on vacation in the Bahamas, enjoying a swim in the ocean when a phone call from the president of a country called Korea was received. President Kim had called to request that Soros come and contribute his expertise.

By the time Soros arrived in Korea, nearly every business had already collapsed, leaving him with no real partner company to rebuild the economy. He expressed great reluctance. After examining the current state and condition of the many companies in Korea, he deemed the Daesung Group the most stable and reliable partner. A meeting was arranged at the Chosun Hotel, where Younghoon and the youngest of all you, Sung Joo, accompanied me to meet with Soros. He expressed his interest in collaborating with the Daesung Group and made a couple of proposals: to acquire one of the Korean banks and to acquire and operate a brokerage. I could

업이 무너질 때 유리한 조건으로 주식을 사고 국가와 기업이 회복되는 시점에서 되파는 방법으로, 단기간에 큰 금액을 확보하는 방식의 사업 형태를 추구했다. 그런 사업은 많은 사람들의 고통을 담보로 하지 않을 수 없다. 내가 보기에 그의 제안은 공익과 환경을 중요시하는 우리 기업이념과는 어울리지 않았다. 나는 그의 제안을 거절하였다.

그때 죠지 소로스는 무척 당황하는 모습이었다. 세계 금융의 황제로 인정받고 있고 더욱이 대통령이 직접 요청하여 외화가 바닥난 한국에 왔는데, 대성그룹 회장이 같이 일을 하지 않겠다고 하니 적잖이 놀랄 수밖에 없었다. 죠지 소로스는 영훈이를 뉴욕에 불러서 나를 설득해주길 원했다. 미국의 자택에 영훈이를 초대하여 함께 식사도 하고 자신이 수집해 놓은 예술품도 감상하는 기회를 갖자고 했다. 하지만 내가 가지 말라고 하여 영훈이가 순종하고 가지 않은 것을 고맙게 생각하고 있다.

not easily accept his investment proposals, for I did not agree with his investment approach of buying stocks when a national economy or large business was in relapse, only to resell the stocks when the economy or business recovered. In other words, he was interested in making large profits in a short period of time before slipping away. To me, his investment approach would only succeed at the expense of others' loss. I declined Soros' proposal. I felt his approach contradicted the Daesung Group's pursuit for the common good.

Soros had a look of utter shock and confusion on his face. After all, he was the world-renowned king of finance and had come to Korea upon the urgent request of the Korean president to help the Korean currency recover. Yet there I was, the chairman of the Daesung Group, declining this man's offer to help. Upon returning to New York, Soros sent Younghoon an invitation to his private home to join him for dinner and to see his private collection of art works. It was an effort, I believe, to ask Younghoon to convince me to agree to establishing a partnership with him. Younghoon did not accept Soros' invitation because I had asked him not to go. I was very grateful that Younghoon had followed my wishes.

7. 어두울 때 더욱 빛난 하나님의 영광

　　IMF기간 중에 그런 초대가 참 많았다. 영훈이는 그때 내게 상황이 가장 어두울 때 하나님의 영광이 가장 밝게 드러난다는 사실을 말해주었다. 다른 대기업들이 하루가 멀다 하고 무너져 내릴 때, 대성그룹은 미래를 예측하는 준비된 기업으로 각광을 받게 되었다. 영훈이는 이사야 60장 1절에서 3절을 자주 인용했다.

"일어나라 빛을 발하라

이는 네 빛이 이르렀고

여호와의 영광이 네 위에 임하였음이니라.

보라 어둠이 땅을 덮을 것이며,

캄캄함이 만민을 가리려니와

오직 여호와께서 네 위에 임하실 것이며,

그의 영광이 네 위에 나타나리니

나라들은 네 빛으로

왕들은 비치는 네 광명으로 나아오리라."

　　죠지 소로스가 찾아온 것도 영훈이는 이러한 맥락에서 이해했다. 신문에서만 보던 유명한 사람이 찾아와서 같이 일할

7. God's Shining Glory in the Midst of Darkness

During the financial crisis, we received several invitations for partnership. Younghoon reminded me that God's glory shines brightest in the midst of greatest hardship and darkness. To all the other businesses, which were collapsing one by one, tomorrow seemed so distant but the Daesung Group was in the spotlight as a business equipped for a promising future. Younghoon frequently recited the following Scripture verses:

> [1] *Arise, shine, for your light has come,*
> *and the glory of the LORD rises upon you.*
> [2] *See, darkness covers the earth and thick darkness is over the*
> *peoples, but the LORD rises upon you*
> *and his glory appears over you.*
> [3] *Nations will come to your light, and kings to the*
> *brightness of your dawn.*
> *(Isaiah 60:1-3)*

We could not help but feel honored that someone as famous as George Soros, someone whom we had only read about in newspapers, had approached the Daesung Group with wishes to collaborate in a partnership. Though in the end we declined Soros' proposal, I believe our encounter with him was an excellent experience.

Despite the unfavorable conditions, Younghoon took on

사람으로 우리를 선택했다고 하니, 한편으로는 영광스러운 면이 없지 않았다. 대성그룹이 추구한 공익성에 부합되지 않아 거절했지만 우리에게는 참 좋은 경험이 되었다.

그 어려운 때에 회사의 모든 부서를 책임지고 리더십을 발휘한 영훈이로 인해 대성그룹은 순조롭게 성장해갈 수 있었다. 모두 영훈이의 탁월한 경영능력과 신실한 신앙의 결과라고 생각한다. 나는 그런 영훈이를 볼 때마다 너무나도 기쁘고 든든했다. 영훈이는 그 모든 것을 항상 하나님의 은혜라고 겸손히 말했다.

full responsibility over all sectors and divisions of the Daesung Group, and through his strong leadership, the Daesung Group was able to further advance and develop smoothly. I believe our success is a result of Younghoon's excellent business management skills and sincere faith in the Lord. Younghoon always speaks humbly of how all that is good is a display of God's grace. Every time I look at Younghoon, I feel great happiness and a sense of assurance.

8. 50년을 하루같이 지켜주신 하나님의 은혜

한국의 에너지산업은 국제사회의 에너지산업 역사와 맥을 같이 한다. 즉 고체인 석탄에서 시작하여 액체인 석유를 거쳐 기체인 천연가스의 단계를 거치며 발전해 왔다. 그 과정에서 대성그룹은 미래를 예측하고 한발 앞서 달려왔다. 창립 50주년을 맞았을 때 대성그룹은 이제 한국의 에너지산업을 이끄는 자리에 우뚝 서게 되었다. 시작은 극히 미약한 모습이었고 성장하는 과정에서 첩첩 산중을 넘어야 하는 어려움이 잇달았다. 하지만 그 모든 과정에 함께 하신 하나님의 은혜로 세계 속에 초우량 기업으로 발돋움하여 대성그룹의 100주년을 희망차게 바라볼 수 있는 자리에 이른 것이다.

한국도시가스협회 회장을 두 번 맡아 한국가스업계를 이끌면서 미래의 친환경에너지 연구개발에 나는 많은 관심을 기울여 왔다. 에너지사업 발전에 공헌한 바를 인정받아 1999년 나는 정부로부터 금탑산업훈장을 받는 영광을 얻게 되었다.

8. 50 Years as One Day

Korea's energy industry shares a history with the international energy industry. For instance, the energy industry evolved from the use of coal, then to petroleum, and now to natural gas. And since the beginning of Korea's energy industry, the Daesung Group has always looked far ahead into the future and has been one step ahead. By the time the Group celebrated its 50th anniversary, it had become a leader of Korea's energy industry. Though our beginnings were weak and though we experienced many trials through our journey to the top, God's grace was with us throughout it all. In just 50 years, the Daesung Group has climbed to a position alongside many international enterprises; and from where the Group stands right now, future prospects for the 100th anniversary look bright and hopeful.

While serving two terms as the chairman of the Korea City Gas Association, my interest in research on environmentally friendly energy sources escalated. And for my contribution to the energy industry, the Korean government awarded me with the Golden Tower Industrial Medal of Honor.

9. 임직원들에 대한 사랑과 감사

나는 대성그룹의 임직원들을 항상 내 몸과 같이 사랑하는 마음으로 대해 왔다. 임직원들과 그 가족들을 모두 대성의 한 가족으로 여기고 직원들의 수고에 많은 관심을 가지고 항상 고마운 마음을 표현하고자 노력했다. 그들의 수고와 헌신이 없었다면 대성그룹은 결코 지금처럼 성장하지 못했을 것이다. 특히 회사에서 근무하는 가장을 잘 보필한 직원들의 가족들이 있었기 때문에, 대성의 사업들은 신행하는 분야마다 좋은 결과를 얻을 수 있었다고 생각한다.

IMF 때 많은 회사들이 도산하고 구조조정으로 직원들을 퇴직시키는 긴장된 분위기 속에서 나 또한 회사의 몸집을 줄여야 하는 게 아닌가 생각하지 않을 수 없었다. 그때 영훈이는 대성의 임직원들이 불안과 염려 없이 성실하게 근무할 수 있도록 구조조정을 하지 않도록 조언했다. 나라의 경제가 추락해 갈 때 직원들과 그들의 가족들을 보호하고자 했던 영훈이의 배려로 우리 회사는 구조조정 없이 잘 운영될 수 있었다. 이 또한 하나님의 특별한 은혜였음을 고백하게 된다.

회사가 먼저 직원들을 사랑하는 마음으로 품을 때, 직원들은 회사를 자신의 삶의 터전으로 삼고 애사심을 가지고 업무에 전념할 수 있다. 서로 사랑과 성실로 섬길 수 있는 분위기

9. Thanksgiving and Affection for Employees of the Daesung Group

I have always made an effort to love the Daesung Group employees as myself. Because I consider my employees, and their families, members of a greater family called the Daesung Group, I take great interest in acknowledging their dedication and efforts and in expressing my grateful heart to them. If it weren't for their hard work and devotion to the company, the Daesung Group would not have been able to grow as much as it has. The Group was able to flourish in every aspect and every area because of the families who stood by our employees.

When the financial crisis struck and all businesses began to downsize, laying off countless employees, I could not help considering downsizing the company. Younghoon advised me not to lay off any employees so that they may continue to work with diligence, free from worry or anxiety. While the national economy was collapsing, Younghoon's counsel to protect employees of the Daesung Group, and their families, in the end, contributed to allowing the Group to operate without downsizing. This too, I confess, was a product of God's wonderful grace.

When a company embraces its employees with a loving heart, its employees in turn respond with tremendous loyalty

를 만드는 것이 내가 해야 할 마땅한 도리라고 생각한다. 직원
들과 그들의 가족들이 모두 행복을 누릴 수 있는 기업문화가
대성그룹의 고유한 전통으로 계속 이어져 가기를 소원한다.

to the company and they work with more diligence and devotion than ever. I feel it is my responsibility to make a stable environment for our employees to serve faithfully and with love. It is my earnest hope that the Daesung Group's long tradition of providing joy and happiness for our employees and their families may continue.

Chapter 6
My Last Request
나의
마지막 부탁

금탑훈장을 수상하는 김수근 회장
Receiving the Golden Tower Industrial Medal of
Honor (1999)

김영훈 대구도시가스회장 취임
Younghoon David Kim's inauguration as Chairman of
Daegu City Gas Co., Ltd. (December 28, 2000)

대성그룹 창업주 김수근 회장이 미국 유학 중인 아들 영훈에게 보낸 편지들
Founding Chairman of the Daesung Group
Soo Keun Kim's letters to his son, Younghoon

나의 마지막 부탁

2000년 10월 1일 영훈이의 셋째 아기가 막 태어나려던 무렵, 나는 영훈이를 불러오게 했다. 그때 영훈이에게 하고 싶은 중요한 말을 건네고 싶었기 때문이다. 나의 마지막 부탁을 영훈이가 잘 준행할 줄로 믿는다.

영훈이에게 회사의 미래를 맡긴다고 말한 다음 날, 나는 마지막 생일잔치를 앞두고 마음이 참으로 기뻤다. 내 평생 그렇게 가볍고 기쁜 마음을 기져보기는 처음이었다. 나의 마지막 때를 감지하고 내가 그렇게 사랑하던 사업을 모두 내려놓았을 때 내 마음은 세상이 줄 수 없는 기쁨으로 충만해졌다. 세례 받은 후 그때까지 나는 교회에 집사 직분으로 매주 출석하고 있었다. 그럼에도 불구하고 나는 그리스도께서 내 삶의 주인이 되신다고 인정하기에는 너무나도 강한 자아를 버리지 못하고 있었다. 항상 내가 모든 결정의 주체가 되어 왔다. 그러나 내가 강하게 붙들고 있던 사업에 대한 집착을 모두 내려놓았을 때 나는 하늘로부터 내려오는 폭포수와 같은 기쁨을 누릴 수 있었다. 그날 너희들도 내가 어린아이 같은 모습으로 기뻐하는 것을 보고 모두 무척 즐거워하였지. 그것은 바로 거듭난 자만이 누리는 그런 기쁨이었다.

나는 이제 내 이야기를 마쳐야 할 것 같다. 나도 모든 사람

My Last Request

On October 1, 2000, at around the time Younghoon's third child was born, I asked him to come over, for I had been longing to share a few special words with him. I wished to make one last request to him, certain that he would follow my instructions.

The day after I expressed my wishes for Younghoon to assume leadership of the Daesung Group, I celebrated my last birthday. My heart was filled with unspeakable joy. I had never before felt so lighthearted and joyous. My heart overflowed with a joy that nothing of this world could ever come close to bringing when I recognized that it was time for me to let go of the company that I had loved for so long. I had faithfully attended Sunday services since the day I was baptized and had served as a deacon, but I had not been able to declare God as the author of my life because of my strong sense of self. I had always been the main decision-maker in my life, but at the moment I released the firm grip I had on the company, I experienced uncontainable joy that cascaded like waterfalls from heaven above. You, my children, took joy in seeing my emotions overflow with a childlike happiness. The joy I experienced that day was a joy that is felt only by those who have been born again.

I have now reached the end of what I have to say. It is now

이 가는 그 길을 따라 하나님께로 돌아갈 시간이 되었다. 아비가 너희들에게 남겨놓은 일들을 잘 부탁한다. 천국에서 만나자. 그 기쁜 곳에서 나는 너희들을 기다릴 것이다. 이날 내가 영훈이와 함께 생전 처음으로 예수님을 주님으로 모시는 기도를 기쁘게 드렸기에 이제 천국에서 영원히 주님과 기쁘게 살 것을 조금도 의심하지 않는다.

"살아계신 하나님 우리 아버지!
이제까지 주님을 알지 못하고
선하신 주님을 떠나 죄 가운데 방황했던
저의 모든 죄를 회개하고 자복합니다.
방황하던 저를
주님께서 불쌍히 여기시고
오래 참아주심을 감사드립니다.
이제 예수 그리스도께서
십자가에서 흘리신 보혈의 은혜를 믿고
주님께서 부활하심으로 허락하신 영생을 믿고
주님 앞에 나옵니다.
주님께서 약속하신 죄 사함과 영생을
저에게 주시고,

time for me to follow the path that leads to God. Please take to heart my last requests. May we meet again in heaven. I will be waiting for you, my children, in God's perfect kingdom. Because of this prayer that I prayed with Younghoon—a prayer I had never before prayed—I do not doubt for a moment that I will enter the gates of heaven and live eternally in joy with our Lord.

Living God, my Father!

Forgive me Lord, for I had not known you.

I confess and repent all the sins I committed,

lost in sin and away from Your faithfulness.

I thank you, Lord, for your compassion and patience.

I believe in the precious blood of Jesus that was

shed on the cross for me;

I believe I have redemption through

the resurrection of Christ.

And now I come to you my Lord.

Grant me the forgiveness of sins

and the eternal life you promised to all who believe;

Send the Holy Spirit to guide me

on this path towards you Lord;

지금부터 천국 가서 주님을 뵈올 때까지
저에게 성령을 보내사
한 걸음 한 걸음 주님과 동행하게 하여 주시옵소서.
주님께서 허락하신 구원의 은혜를 감사드리며
이 모든 말씀을 우리의 주가 되시는
예수님 거룩하신 이름을 받들어
간절히 기도드립니다. 아—멘."

May I walk with Jesus each step of the way.

I thank you, Lord, for your saving grace.

I pray all these things

in the holy name of my Lord Jesus Christ.

Amen.

Chapter 7

Chairman Younghoon David Kim's Role and Vision

김영훈 회장의
역할과 비전

김영훈 대성그룹 회장 제8대, 제9대 한국도시가스협회 회장 취임
Chairman Younghoon David Kim's inaugural ceremonies as the 8th
and 9th chairman of the Korea City Gas Association

세계에너지회의 부회장 주제강연
Delivering a keynote speech
as Vice Chairman of
the World Energy Council(WEC)
(October 2006)

대구 LFG 준공
Completion of
the LFG landfill in Daegu
(November 29, 2006)

부산 APEC 부시 대통령
With U.S. President
George W. Bush at
the APEC Summit held
in Busan, Korea (2005)

다보스 북핵 패널 발표
Davos World Economic
Forum (WEF) North
Korean Nuclear Problem
Panel Discussion
(January 2004)

2002년 APEC
러시아 푸틴 대통령과 대담
With Russian President
Vladimir Putin at the
2002 APEC Summit

사회 순화 기능 입증한
'말아톤' 제작 참여
Marathon proved the
growing potential of
the film industry (2005)

뉴질랜드 헬렌 클락 수상과
영화산업 협력 약속
Agreement for
cooperation in the film
industry established
with Prime Minister
Helen Clark of
New Zealand(2005)

Park Road Post 영화사와
Black Sheep 투자 조인식
Black Sheep Investment Signing
Ceremony with Park Road Post
(October 11, 2005)

아카데미 수상자
웨타영화사 리챠드 테일러와
MOU 체결
MOU with five-time
Academy Award winner
Richard Taylor of Weta
Worshop (July 14, 2006)

한국·몽골 경제협력회의
Joint-meeting of
the Korea-Mongolia
Economic Cooperation
Committee (May 2006)

몽골 바가반디 대통령으로로부터
몽골 명예영사로 임명됨
Appointed honorary
consul of Mongolia by
Mongolian President
Natsagiyn Bagabandi

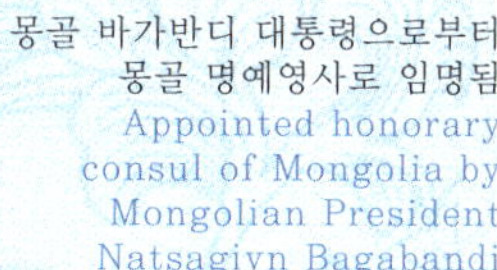

몽골 두레고비프로젝트 시설
설치
Installation of
the DURE-Gobi Project
facilities in Mongolia
(2002)

숭찌엔 부수상 면담
With Chinese Deputy
Prime Minister (1998)

중국 NDRC 마카이 주임
With Chairman Ma Kai
of China's National
Development and Reform
Commission (NDRC)
(August 29, 2006)

중국 에너지 부주임 쟝크바우
With Vice Chairman of
China's NDRC,
Zhang Guo Bao (2006)

2011년 세계육상대회 유치
Successful bid for Daegu to host
the 2011 IAAF World Championships in Athletics

대구국제육상경기대회
International track event
held in Daegu (2006)

대성그룹, 대구도시가스,
코리아닷컴 후원
International track
event sponsored by
the Daesung Group,
Daegu City Gas, and
Korea.com

1. 아버지의 마지막 당부

6장까지 아버지 회고록의 편집을 마치고, 이 책의 편집자로서 나는 대성그룹의 미래를 향해 그룹의 세계화를 실현해 나가고 있는 김영훈 회장의 활동과 비전으로 이 책을 마무리하는 것이 필요함을 느낀다.

나의 아버지는 긍정적이고 적극적이며 보수적이면서도 한편으로는 매우 진취적인 분이셨다. 나는 아버지같이 명석한 분을 만나본 적이 없다. 매사에 의욕이 강하시던 아버지께서 폐암 진단을 받으시고 더 이상 치료가 불가능함을 들으셨을 때 얼마나 실망이 크셨겠는가!

그 후 아버지께서는 의사였던 친구의 민간 요법에 의존하셨다. 그러던 중 2000년 10월 1일, 그토록 애착을 가지셨던 모든 사업에 대한 집착을 내려놓으시고, 천국에 가실 준비를 하시면서 김영훈 회장에게 마지막 말씀을 하셨다. 평소 건강하셨을 때 회사의 주요 업무를 전적으로 김영훈 회장에게 위임하신 아버지께서 장래 회사의 모든 일들을 잘 책임져 달라는 당부 말씀을 남겨주신 것이다.

그 다음날 아버지의 마지막 생신을 축하해 드리기 위해 모든 가족이 모였다. 하시던 사업에 지극히 큰 애정을 보이셨던 것을 우리 자녀들은 잘 알고 있었다. 그날 모든 것을 내려놓으

1. Father's Last Remarks

I have now reached the end of editing my father's memoirs. As the editor of this book, I feel it necessary to conclude this book with brief mentions of Chairman Younghoon David Kim's role and vision in leading the Daesung Group towards full-fledged globalization.

My father was optimistic, enthusiastic and, though conservative at times, progressive in many ways. I have never met anyone as clever as my father. I can't imagine how disappointed and shocked he must have been when he was diagnosed with lung cancer and received news that it was too late for treatment, especially because he was always so energetic.

When he was diagnosed with cancer, Father decided to turn to a doctor friend of his, who recommended various folk remedies, for help. On October 1, 2000, Father decided to release his stronghold on his company and prepare for eternity, and he made his last request to my brother Younghoon, asking him to assume full responsibility over the company, which he had directly managed for so many years when he was healthy.

The entire family gathered the next day to celebrate Father's last birthday. All of us children were well aware of Father's tremendous affection and attachment to his company.

시고 진심으로 하늘의 소망을 바라보시며 기뻐하시는 아버지 모습을 뵐 수 있었던 것은 놀라운 기적이었다. 어머니와 우리 자녀들이 하나님께 기도드린 평생의 간구가 응답 받은 날이었다. 아버지께서 그토록 하늘나라의 소망을 가지시고 즐거워하시는 모습을 나는 처음 보았다.

죄 가운데 태어난 우리 인간은 거룩한 하나님 앞에서는 전적으로 타락한 피조물일 뿐이다. 열정을 다해 사업을 하셨던 아버지로서는 이 진리를 받아들이는 것이 쉽지 않았다. 그러나 그의 마지막 생신 잔치였던 2000년 10월 2일, 아버지는 김영훈 회장과 함께 예수 그리스도를 주님으로 영접하는 기도를 진지하게 드리셨다. 그리고 그 기도가 아버지의 마지막 기도가 되었다.

거듭난 기쁨으로 충만하던 아버지께서는 두 달 후 2001년 새해 첫날 오후에 의식을 잃으셨다. 마침 김영훈 회장은 그의 둘째 딸 은진이가 맹장염으로 밤새 앓다가 복막염이 되어 새해 벽두에 수술을 하게 되었기에, 아버지께 손녀 딸의 수술이 잘 되었다고 기쁘게 말씀드렸다. "아버지! 지난 밤에 딸아이를 하나님께서 위기에서 구원해 주셨어요." 그때 아버지는 "그래, 그래." 하시며 참 기뻐하셨다. 그날 오후 아버지는 의식을 잃고 다시 정신을 회복하지 못하셨고 2001년 2월 20일 천국에 가셨다.

Seeing Father lay down all his attachments, sincerely look to the hope of heaven, and rejoice with all his heart was a miracle in itself. That day, God answered the lifelong prayers of my mother and all my siblings. It was the first time I had seen my father rejoice with such an incredible hope of heaven.

Before our holy God we are no more than sinful creatures born in sin. To my father, a man who had devoted all his passions to his business, this truth was something he could not accept. But on October 2, 2000, Father prayed with Younghoon for his salvation and accepted Christ as His Savior.

With overflowing joy in his heart, Father lost consciousness months later in the afternoon on January 1, 2001. Younghoon's daughter Eun Jin suffered all New Year's Eve with appendicitis and finally had to have surgery. The surgery was successful. He rushed to Father to share with him the good news: "Father! God was by Eun Jin's side all throughout the night. He saved her life!" And Father joyously replied, "Good, good." And he lost consciousness that very night, on New Year's Day, and later passed away on February 20, 2001.

2. 다시 뛴 아버지의 심장

아버지가 천국에 가시던 날에 참으로 놀라운 일이 있었다. 의식을 잃으시고 소천하시기까지 50일간 매일 가족들이 서로 번갈아 가며 하루 종일 아버지 병실을 지켰다. 그날도 김영훈 회장은 병원에서 아버지를 뵙고 잠시 저녁 식사를 하러 세브란스병원을 나와 연세대학교 앞 로터리를 돌아가는데 핸드폰으로 아버지께서 임종하셨다는 사실을 듣게 되었다. 급히 차를 돌려 병실에 도착했을 때 아버지의 심전도는 완전히 멈춰 있었다.

김영훈 회장은 하나님께 간절히 기도를 드렸다. 사업에 대한 집착이 너무나 강하셨던 아버지께서는 늘 일을 더 하고 싶어 하셨다. 그러한 아버지께서 하늘나라에 가실 준비가 아직도 완전히 되지 않았다는 생각이 들어 김영훈 회장은 하나님께 부르짖었다. "하나님! 우리 아버지를 지금 이대로 부르신다면, 꼭 천국에서 받아주세요." 간절히 기도드리던 중에 기적이 일어났다. 멈추었던 심전도가 다시 뛰기 시작한 것이다. 약 30분간 다시 뛰더니 그 다음에 멈추면서 아버지는 영원히 천국에 가셨다.

그때 김영훈 회장은 아버지께서 "영훈아, 안심해라."는 말씀을 전해주시려고 잠시 돌아왔다가 가셨음을 확신하였다. 평

2. Hearing Father's Heartbeat Again

I witnessed yet another miracle on the day that Father went to heaven. For the fifty days since the day he lost consciousness up until the time he ascended to heaven, the members of our family took turns keeping him company by his bedside at the hospital. It was Younghoon's turn to look after him. Younghoon left Severance Hospital just briefly to grab a quick dinner, when suddenly he received a call that Father's last moments were fast approaching. He quickly turned the car around and rushed to the hospital. When he arrived, Father's heartbeat had already stopped.

Younghoon prayed a most sincere prayer to God. He wasn't certain of whether Father, a man who had devoted his every strength and passion to his company, was prepared to enter the gates of heaven. Younghoon cried out to God, "Lord Father! If it is your will to call him right now, I ask that you receive him in heaven." While praying and crying out to God, a miracle happened. Father's heart began to pulsate again as if to say, "Younghoon! Be at ease." It was as though Father had momentarily returned to have one last chance to share a loving conversation with Younghoon. Father's heart beat for nearly thirty minutes before it stopped again for good; he finally left this earth to live in heaven for eternity.

Father never stopped cherishing and loving Younghoon.

소에 항상 사랑으로 나누시던 대화를 마지막으로 조금 더 하시려고 말이다. 아버지께서는 모든 면에서 김영훈 회장을 무척 아끼고 사랑하셨다. 김영훈 회장도 또한 아버지를 마음 중심으로 사랑하며 늘 존경했다. 김영훈 회장은 아버지께서 바른 길을 가실 때 힘을 실어드리고, 연로하셔서 판단이 흔들리실 때는 충심으로 직언해 올리는 것을 아끼지 않았다.

He too loved and respected Father with all his heart. Younghoon took it to heart to encourage Father whenever he was walking on the straight path, and Younghoon never hesitated to advise him with filial love when his later years began to cloud his judgment.

3. 대성그룹의 미래

　김영훈 회장이 대성그룹의 기획조정실장을 맡았던 10년 동안 우리 그룹의 매출은 3천억 원에서 3조 원으로 크게 성장하였다. 이러한 매출의 괄목할만한 성장은 아버지와 김영훈 회장이 함께 경영의 전문화와 경영의 합리화를 지속적으로 추구한 노력의 결과였다. 김영훈 회장은 기조실장으로서 그룹의 경영방침상 경영의 전문화, 합리화와 함께 세계화를 가장 중요한 경영지표로 삼았다. 이러한 경영방침은 대성그룹 창업주이신 아버지 김수근 회장님께서 늘 추구하시던 것을 이어받은 것이다. 생전에 경영의 전문화와 합리화를 이루신 아버지는 대성그룹의 세계화는 미래를 맡게 된 김영훈 회장의 몫으로 남겨 두셨다. 세계화란 글로벌 스탠다드(Global Standard)가 우리의 스탠다드가 되며 또한 우리의 스탠다드가 글로벌 스탠다드(Global Standard)가 되는 것을 의미한다.

　김영훈 회장은 Ten Ten Ten Plan을 대성그룹 미래의 청사진으로 내걸고 있다. 즉 2010년까지 10조 원 매출에 10억 달러의 순익을 창출하겠다는 것이다. 각 사업부는 9개의 소그룹으로 나뉘어 이 목표를 달성하기 위해 세계 각국에 진출하면서 사업장마다 매출의 증대와 이익의 극대화를 위해 노력하고 있다.

　에너지와 문화사업을 주축으로 하는 20여 개의 계열사들

3. The Future of the Daesung Group

During the ten years that Younghoon headed the Office of Planning and Administration at the Daesung Group, the Group's sales skyrocketed from 300 billion won to 3 trillion won. Such an eye-opening increase in profits was possible because of the combined expertise of my father and Younghoon and their strong management partnership. As the head of the Group's Office of Planning and Administration, Younghoon identified as its top management indexes: expertise in management, rationalization of management, and globalization of management. Such management policies were daily pursued and emphasized by Father. When still alive, he established the former two policies, and he left Younghoon the task of implementing globalization. Through globalization, not only would global standards become our Group's standards, but our Group's standards could become global standards.

The Daesung Group will advance under the blueprint of what Chairman Younghoon David Kim refers to as the "Ten, Ten, Ten Plan," through which the Group hopes to bring about, by 2010, 10 *jo* won (10 billion dollars) in sales and 10 *eok* (1 billion) dollars in profits. To reach this goal, each of the Group's subsidiary departments has been working closely with other major business initiatives of the Group and

은 (CEM)³으로 압축해 볼 수 있다. 즉 첫 C·E·M은 3대 주력 사업군으로 정보통신 (Communications), 에너지 (Energy), 그리고 금융 (Money) 분야를 포괄하고 있다. 세부적으로 보면, 정보통신 (Communications) 사업부에는 대성글로벌네트웍과 코리아닷컴 커뮤니케이션스, 그리고 알파서비스, 베타서비스, 감마서비스가 있다. 에너지 (Energy) 사업으로 대구도시가스, 경북도시가스, 대성싱가폴이 있다. 그리고 금융 (Money) 사업으로 바이넥스트창투사와 ACTS 투자자문회사가 있다.

두번째 C·E·M은 핵심사업군으로 건설 (Construction), 환경 (Environment) 그리고 유통 (Marketing) 사업분야를 포괄하고 있다. 건설 (Construction) 사업으로 RNR 건설이 있고, 환경 (Environment) 사업으로는 대구에너지환경, 대성청정연구소가 있다. 또한 유통 (Marketing) 사업분야에는 글로리아트레이딩과 대성차이나, 웰베이 (Well-Bay) 유통사업부가 있다.

세번째 C·E·M은 전략사업군으로 콘텐츠 (Contents), 교육 (Education), 그리고 미디어 (Media) 사업분야를 포괄한다. 콘텐츠 (Contents) 사업으로 대성닷컴이 있으며 교육사업에는 EU-Learning 사업부, 대성해강과학문화재단과 해강대성장학재단이 있다. 미디어 (Media) 사업으로 시나이미디어

entering foreign markets around the globe, all to increase sales and maximize profits.

The Group's twenty-some subsidiaries are divided into three clusters under the notion of CEM[3]. The first CEM cluster includes the Group's key industries: Communications, Energy, and Money. The Communications sector includes Daesung Global Network Co., Ltd.; Korea.com Communications; Alpha Service Co., Ltd.; Beta Service Co., Ltd.; and Gamma Service Co., Ltd. The Energy sector includes Daegu City Gas Co., Ltd.; and Gyeongbuk City Gas Co., Ltd. The Money sector includes BiNEXT CAPiTAL Co., Ltd.; and Acts Capital Management Co., Ltd.

The second CEM cluster includes the Group's core industries: Construction, Environment, and Marketing. The Construction sector includes RNR Engineering & Construction Co., Ltd. The Environment sector includes Daegu Energy & Environment Co., Ltd.; and the Daesung Institute for Clean Energy. And the Marketing sector includes Gloria Trading Co.,Ltd.; Daesung China Co., Ltd.; and Wellbay.

The third CEM cluster includes the Group's strategic industries: Contents, Education, and Media. The Contents sector includes Daesung.com Co., Ltd. The Education sector includes the EU-Learning Department; the Daesung Haegang Science and Culture Foundation; and the Haegang Daesung Scholarship Foundation. The Media sector includes Sinai

가 있다.

각 계열사는 다양한 분야에서 (CEM)[3]의 시너지 효과를 최대한 발휘하여 대성그룹을 세계적인 초일류 우량 선진기업으로 키우기 위해서 최선을 다하고 있다. 대성그룹은 "마음도 따뜻하게 몸도 따뜻하게" 라는 모토를 기업의 기본 이념으로 내걸고, "고객중심주의"를 경영이념의 기본으로 삼고 있다. 그리하여 고객을 사랑하는 기업, 고객이 사랑하는 기업이 되고자 한마음으로, 한몸이 되어 열심히 노력하고 있다.

이제 대성그룹은 60주년을 맞이하고 있다. 5월에는 World Energy Forum을 개최하며 10월에는 Global Contents Forum을 준비하고 있다. 이를 통해서 우리 기업이 추구하는 두 가지 주력사업, 곧 에너지사업과 문화사업을 세계화하는 계기로 삼고자 하고 있다. 대성그룹의 미래의 청사진을 그려보면서, 이제까지 함께하신 하나님께서 미래에도 함께 해주실 것을 믿는다. 이제까지 대성그룹을 놀랍게 축복하신 하나님께서 앞으로 한결같이 축복하셔서서 100주년이 되는 2047년에는 우리 그룹이 인류사회의 평화와 번영에 크게 기여하는 Global Leader로서 우뚝 설 것을 믿는다,

Media Co., Ltd.

All the Daesung Group subsidiary departments are combining efforts to maximize synergy under the CEM[3] model and are contributing to raising the Group to a world-class global enterprise. The Daesung Group operates under a client-based motto, "Warming Hearts, Warming Bodies," and strives to march forward with one heart and one body to become an enterprise that loves and is loved by its clients.

The Daesung Group has already reached its 60th anniversary milestone. We will be hosting the World Energy Forum this month in May and the Global Contents Forum in October. And through such events the Group hopes to further implement globalization of the Group's operations in the energy and culture industries. Chairman Younghoon David Kim has mentioned many times before, in drawing the blueprints of the future of the Daesung Group, how he is filled with faith that God, Who has been with the Group since the beginning, will continue to lead us in the future. He trusts that God will continue to shower His incredible blessings on the Daesung Group and that by the Group's 100th anniversary in 2047, the Group will have attained status as a global leader that fosters peace and prosperity for humanity.

4. 열방을 기업으로 주리라

이 말씀에서 하나님은 이방 나라들이 그리스도를 믿고, 하나님 품으로 돌아오게 하실 것을 말씀하신다. 대학생활 중 김영훈 회장은 이 말씀 속에서 장차 그가 살아야 할 삶의 비전을 받았다. 그가 바라보고 가꾸어야 할 땅은 그가 태어난 한국뿐만 아니라 온 세계임을 바라보게 하는 말씀이었다.

그에게 주신 재능과 자원을 열심히 개발하기 위해 김영훈 회장은 서울 법대를 졸업한 후 미국의 미시간대학 대학원에서 국제법학과 국제금융을, 그리고 2년간 시티은행에서 실무를 익힌 후 하버드대학 대학원에서 국제경제학과 목회신학을 공부했다. 적극적으로 국제사회에 참여하여 하나님의 공의와 사랑의 다스리심을 온 세계에 전하는 데 쓰임 받기 위해서 그는 최선을 다해 열심히 쥬비하였다.

김영훈 회장은 하나님께서 조용히 그에게 하시는 말씀에 늘 순종하려고 노력한다. "영훈아, 이제 너는 나와 힘을 합하여 선을 이루자." 아브라함은 75세에 부르심을 받고 175세를

4. The Nations, My Inheritance

[8]Ask of me, and I will make the nations your inheritance,
the ends of the earth your possession.
(Psalm 2:8)

This Scripture verse speaks of how all nations and tongues will believe in Christ and return to the arms of God. When Younghoon was attending university, God gave him a vision and purpose through this Bible verse. God opened his eyes to see beyond our mother country, Korea, and look to the world as his arena.

In order to develop the skills and talents that God gave him, Younghoon studied law at Seoul National University, and he later studied international business and comparative law at the University of Michigan Graduate School. After gaining two-years' experience as the assistant manager at Citibank in Seoul, he studied international economics at Harvard University Graduate School and later studied theology at Harvard Divinity School. He spent many years preparing for his path as God's instrument of love and justice in the international arena.

The Lord God quietly said to him, "Younghoon, together let us carry out the good fight on to completion." Abraham

향유함으로써 100년 동안 이 땅에서 하나님과 동행하며 사
는 축복, 곧 영생의 복을 받았다. 아브라함처럼 그리스도를
믿고 하나님과 동행하는 삶 곧 영생을 살도록 부르심을 받은
것을 깨닫고 김영훈 회장은 전심으로 믿음의 경주에 힘을 쏟
고 있다.

received God's call at the age of seventy-five and lived 175 years, walking 100 blessed years on earth with the Lord and receiving everlasting life. My greatest hope is that Chairman Younghoon David Kim, like Abraham, may continue to live a life worthy of God's call, walking daily with Christ and persevering in the race of faith with the hope of eternal life.

5. 한국도시가스협회 회장, WEC 세계 부회장으로 피선

2004년 6월 15일, 한국도시가스협회 회장으로 20주년 행사를 주관하면서 김영훈 회장은 무척 감회가 깊었다. 아버지께서 쓰시던 집무실에서 대성그룹 회장의 중책을 맡고 있는 중에 한국도시가스협회 2대·3대 회장을 역임하신 아버지를 이어 8대·9대 회장을 역임하게 되었기 때문이다. 이것이 모두 하나님의 은혜임을 김영훈 회장은 깊이 깨닫고 있다.

아버지께서는 매년 신년사에서 대성그룹을 세계적인 초일류 우량기업으로 키우고자 하시는 소망을 나누셨다. 이제 그 소망이 김영훈 회장의 국제적 활동을 통해서 현실로 나타나고 있음을 진심으로 감사드린다. 2005년 김영훈 회장은 세계에너지 정책기구인 World Energy Council(이하 WEC)의 아시아태평양지역 부회장으로 선출되어 세계 에너지정책의 방향과 입안을 자문하고 있다. 2006년 10월 30일부터 11월 1일까지 서울에서 개최한 WEC 아시아지역회의에서 주제 강연과 함께 회의를 주재하였다.

김영훈 회장은 에너지 자원이 투기 자본에 의해 요동치지 않도록 제도적 장치를 마련하여 세계 경제를 안정시키고자 하는 제안을 발표하여 국제적인 공감대를 조성할 수 있었다. 이를 실행으로 옮기기 위해서 중국의 에너지산업을 대표하는 장

5. Elected Chairman of the Korea City Gas Association
and Vice Chairman of the World Energy Council (WEC)

On June 15, 2004, Chairman Younghoon David Kim was extremely delighted to be able to celebrate the 20th anniversary of the Korea City Gas Association. It was a special moment for him and for our family because Father was the 2nd and 3rd chairman of the association. And now, following in his footsteps, Younghoon was appointed the 8th and 9th chairman of the association. All this, we know, is a work of God's amazing grace.

Every year in his New Year's message, Father expressed his hopes to see the Daesung Group develop into a world-class, top-ranking enterprise. We are truly grateful that his wishes have now become a reality through Younghoon's activities in the international arena. In 2005, Younghoon was elected Vice Chairman of the World Energy Council (WEC) Asia-Pacific Region and has since helped draft international energy policies and frameworks. He was a keynote speaker at the WEC Asia-Pacific Region Forum, which was held in Seoul from October 30 to November 1 in 2006.

Younghoon proposed a new framework that would ensure energy resources do not fluctuate in accordance with fluctuations in capital flow, and that would secure the global economy. And for this proposal he received international

궈바우 NDRC 대표와 마카이 주석을 만나 중요한 의견들을
나누었다. 또한 2013년에 5,000명의 에너지 전문가들이 모이
는WEC 총회의 한국 유치도 적극 추진하고 있다.

recognition. In order to discuss ways to initiate the framework, he had a meeting with Chairman Ma Kai of the National Development and Reform Commission (NDRC), China's leading economic management agency. Younghoon is currently preparing for the Korean bid to host the 2013 WEC Forum at which more than 5,000 energy experts will gather to draw a road map for the future of the energy industry.

6. 신재생에너지 연구 개발

대성그룹 김영훈 회장은 환경친화적인 에너지를 중심으로 미래 에너지산업이 발전할 것을 예측하고 대성청정에너지연구소를 통해 연구개발에 적극적으로 임하면서 국제적으로 인정받는 신재생에너지 개발에 전력을 쏟고 있다. 그러한 사업의 일환으로 2002년 에너지 빈국인 몽골에 태양력·풍력 복합발전 시스템인 솔라윈 시스템을 설치하여 고비사막지대의 강한 풍력과 넘치는 태양열을 이용하여 선기를 생산해낼 수 있었다. 몽골의 고비사막에서 발생하는 황사현상은 현재 미국 서부 지역까지 피해를 주고 있다. 김영훈 회장은 황사로 인한 고통을 해결하기 위해서는 반드시 고비사막 녹화를 추진해야 할 것을 예측하고, 대성의 에너지 기술력이 그러한 녹화사업에 견인차 역할을 하도록 노력하고 있다.

2006년 대통령 국빈 방문 시 한·몽 경제협력위원회가 울란바토르에서 열렸다. 그때 김영훈 회장은 한·몽경제협력위원회 회장으로서 황사방지를 위한 솔라윈 시스템을 주 테마로 하는 에너지공원을 만들어 고비사막 녹화를 가능하게 히는 프로젝트를 제안했다. 몽골당국은 대성그룹이 앞장서서 이 프로젝트를 현실화시켜 주길 요청하였다. 이를 위해 울란바토르에 100만 평의 땅을 제공하는 등 매우 적극적인 뜻을 전해왔다.

6. Research on Renewable Energy

The Daesung Group believes that the future of the energy industry will focus on environmentally friendly, renewable energy sources. Thus the Daesung Institute of Clean Energy continues with its diligent efforts to discover renewable energy sources that will, indeed, gain international recognition. In 2002, the Group introduced the SolaWin System—a system that makes efficient use of solar and wind power to create energy—in Mongolia, a country that has a limited supply of energy. We successfully harnessed the strong winds and excessive solar power of the Gobi Desert to create energy. The yellow sand and dust storms of the Gobi Desert are affecting regions as far away as North America. It is absolutely critical that effective afforestation measures be carried out in the Gobi Desert, in order to prevent the dangerous outcomes of this process of desertification. To this end, the Daesung Group will continue to contribute its expertise in this area.

The Korea-Mongolia Economic Cooperation Committee gathered in Ulaanbaatar in 2006 during Korean President Moo Hyun Roh's visit to Mongolia. As the chairman of the committee, Younghoon proposed the construction of a renewable energy park, which would incorporate the SolaWin System, in the Gobi Desert to solve the problem of

한·몽경제협력기구를 통해 대성그룹은 몽골과 한국 정부와 함께 이 프로젝트를 실현해 가도록 준비하고 있다.

현재 기후변화 문제는 지구의 생존 자체를 위협하는 수준에 이르고 있다. 북극의 빙하가 급격히 녹아가고 해수면이 빠르게 높아지면서 국가의 존재가 사라질 수 있다는 예측도 가능해졌다. 이에 세계는 교토의정서 기후환경변화협약에 입각하여 CO_2 방출량을 1992년 수준으로 줄이는 데 동의하였다. 기후변화 문제를 해결하기 위해 미국을 비롯한 많은 선진국들이 신재생에너지 개발에 힘을 쏟고 있다. 대성그룹 김영훈 회장은 온실가스 감축과 화석연료 대체에 효과적인 LFG (Land Fill Gas) 사업을 대구 방천리에 성공적으로 추진하여 신재생에너지 개발에 더욱 박차를 가하고 있다.

desertification. Mongolian government officials requested the Daesung Group to take on a leading role in carrying out this proposal. The Mongolian government expressed great interest in this project, notably offering 1 million *pyeong* (3.3 million square meters) of land along the outskirts of Ulaanbaatar. Implementation of the construction of the renewable energy park is currently underway under collaboration between the Daesung Group—via the Korea-Mongolia Economic Cooperation Committee—and the governments of Korea and Mongolia.

Currently, climatic changes throughout the globe are posing serious threats to the very survival of all life. With rapid melting of glaciers in the North Pole and rising sea levels, the possibility of disappearing countries and nations is increasing. We have agreed to reduce CO_2 gas emissions to the 1992 level in accordance with the Kyoto Protocol and the UN Climate Change Convention. Many developed countries, including the U.S., are devoting great efforts towards resolving the climate change problem. The Daesung Group continues to reduce greenhouse-gas emissions through its sanitary landfill in Bangchon-ri and its production of landfill gas (LFG), and is successfully developing new renewable energy sources.

7. 다보스 세계경제포럼

김영훈 회장은 스위스 다보스에서 매년 열리는 세계경제포럼 (World Economic Forum, 이하 WEF)에 패널리스트로 매년 참석하고 있다. WEF에서 세계 정상의 리더들과 정치, 경제, 문화의 주요 현안들에 관해 토론하고 지구촌이 나아가야 할 방향을 제시하고 있다.

5년째 다보스 포럼에 참석하면서, 김영훈 회장은 '다보스 구상'을 한다. 고 이병철 삼성그룹 창업회장이 매년 신년에 '도쿄 구상'을 했던 것처럼 다보스에서 세계 주요 현안들을 조망하며 우리 그룹의 앞날을 설계하고 있다.

특히 지구촌 힘의 균형이 정부 부문에서 민간 부문으로 이전하고 있고 민간의 힘도 다시 세분화되고 있다. 이러한 때 김영훈 회장은 에너지 안보의 우려가 높아지고 있는 현상을 고려하여 민관협력의 새로운 모델을 개발해야 할 때라고 생각한다.

2004년에도 김영훈 회장님은 국제원자력기구 사무총장이자 2005년 노벨평화상 수상자인 엘바라데이와 북핵문제를 주제로 하는 자리에 패널리스트로 참석했다. 미국 상원의원 짐 리치, 캐나다 핵문제 권위자 모리스 스트롱과 함께 유엔군축문제전문가 페트리샤 루이스의 사회로 국제사회의 지도자들과 북핵문제에 관해 토의하면서, 리비아의 카다피처럼 북한을

7. Davos World Economic Forum

Every year, Chairman Younghoon David Kim serves on the panel at the World Economic Forum (WEF), which is held annually in Davos, Switzerland. Worldwide leaders and experts gather at the WEF to discuss key issues surrounding politics, economics, culture, and future directions.

The founding chairman of the Samsung Group, Byung Chul Lee, declared the "Tokyo Plan" in his annual New Year's messages. In a similar way, Younghoon too has dedicated his efforts to the "Davos Plan" for the past five years of attendance at the WEF. To this end, he continues to shed light on key global challenges at Davos and, at the same time, map out the future of the Daesung Group.

We are increasingly witnessing the global transfer of power from government to the private sector and a rise in public-private segmentation. With the onset of such trends, threats against energy security are also on the rise. Younghoon believes we have reached the point in time where we must develop a new model for private cooperation.

In 2004, Younghoon had the opportunity to join a panel discussion regarding issues and challenges around North Korea's nuclear program with the 2005 Nobel Peace Prize recipient Dr. Mohamed El Baradei, who is head of the International Atomic Energy Agency (IAEA). The panelists—

국제사회 속으로 나오도록 유도하자고 제안하여 좋은 반응을 얻었다. 미국 정부가 그 후 북핵문제를 이러한 방향으로 다루어가는 것을 목도하면서 민간기업인의 적극적인 국제회의 참여가 국제사회를 돕는 중요한 통로가 될 수 있음을 볼 수 있었다.

2007년 다보스에서 열린 WEF에서 신재생에너지 문제는 가장 핵심적인 아젠다로 논의되었다. UN 정부간기후변화위원회(IPCC)도 이 문제에 대한 심각한 경고를 담은 공식 문건을 2월 초에 발표하였다. 이번 대성그룹 창립 60주년을 맞아 개최되는 대성글로벌에너지포럼에서 김영훈 회장이 바로 이 이슈(issue)를 주제로 잡은 것은 매우 시기 적절한 것으로 판단된다.

including U.S. Iowan Senator Jim Leach and Canadian nuclear expert Maurice Strong; United Nations arms control expert Patricia Louise, who served as a facilitator; and other world leaders—discussed ways to deal with North Korea's nuclear program. Panelists approved Younghoon's suggestion to help North Korea enter the international community, as was done in the case of Libya. This U.S. government approach towards nuclear disarmament and North Korea's nuclear program has shed light on the pivotal role of private entrepreneurs in contributing to the advancement of the international community.

Renewable energy was at the top of the 2007 Davos WEF agenda. In early February 2007, the UN Intergovernmental Panel on Climate Change (IPCC) expressed also the urgency for the need for renewable energy resources. Younghoon believes the upcoming Daesung World Energy Forum—organized in celebration of the Group's 60th anniversary—comes at a perfect time in history as it will deal with issues surrounding the theme of renewable energy.

8. 차세대 전략산업, 문화산업

　대성그룹 김영훈 회장은 21세기의 차세대 전략산업은 문화산업이라고 예측하였다. 이제까지 자동차, 조선, 철강, 반도체 등의 사업이 효자사업이었다면 문화사업은 미래의 효녀사업이라고 할 수 있다. 세계 문화산업시장은 반도체산업의 시장보다 월등히 크다. 앞으로 김영훈 회장은 문화산업을 누가 주도하느냐에 따라서 기업과 국가의 장래가 달려 있다고 보고 있다.

　전경련 문화산업특별위원회 위원장으로서 김영훈 회장은 한국의 모든 기업이 문화산업의 중요성을 인식하도록 힘쓰고 있다. 계열사 바이넥스트 창투사를 통해서 영화, 게임, 모바일 등에 적극 투자하는 것도 그러한 인식에서 기인한다. 2005년 주위의 우려에도 불구하고 영화 '말아톤'에 투자했다. 장애를 사회가 긍정적으로 이해하도록 돕고 싶은 뜻으로 투자했던 그 영화는 흥행에 크게 성공하였고, 문화가 사회를 순화시킬 수 있다는 큰 가능성을 보여주었다.

　창업 60주년을 맞는 대성그룹은 창립기념일인 5월 10일에 대성세계에너지포럼을 (Daesung World Energy Forum), 10월 10일에는 대성글로벌컨텐츠포럼을 (Daesung Global Contents Forum) 열기로 했다. 컨텐츠 포럼의 주제는

8. Culture Industry, the New Strategic Industry

Chairman Younghoon David Kim deems the strategic industry of the 21st century to be the culture industry. If the automobile, steel, shipbuilding, and semiconductor industries were the filial sons of the past generations, the culture industry is the filial daughter of the future. The value and vastness of the semiconductor industry market is incomparable to that of the global culture industry. The future of nations and the business world depends on who holds the position of power in the culture industry.

As Chairman of the FKI Special Committee for the Culture Industry, Younghoon strives to help all businesses in Korea recognize the value of the culture industry. Through BiNEXT CAPiTAL Co., Ltd., the Daesung Group invests in films, games, mobile solutions, and other areas in the culture industry. Despite many concerns and objections, the Group invested in the film *Marathon* in 2005. We invested in this particular film because of our wishes to help the greater society better understand and perceive persons with disabilities in a positive light. *Marathon* not only became a major box-office hit, but it also validated the great potential of culture for bringing greater good to society.

In celebration of the Daesung Group's 60th anniversary, the Group will hold its first ever Daesung World Energy

Entertainment as Education이다. 즉 영화, 드라마, 음악 등 문화컨텐츠가 가지는 흡인력을 사용자들의 삶을 활성화시키는 활력소로 승화시켜서 사회환경 개선의 촉매로 활용하고자 하는 대성그룹 김영훈 회장의 의지를 표명하고 있다.

Forum on its anniversary on May 10, 2007, and also the Daesung Global Contents Forum on October 10. The Group has chosen as the theme of the latter forum "Entertainment as Education," in hopes to inform the public of the powerful role of movies, dramas, music, and other culture content in improving our daily lives, and to introduce culture content as a catalyst for educational and social change.

9. APEC, 한국기업 대표로 참석

또한 대성그룹 김영훈 회장은 매년 APEC에 한국기업 대표로 참석하여 아시아 태평양지역의 대통령 및 수상들과 경제 분야 대표들과 만나 에너지뿐만 아니라 정치, 경제, 문화, 환경 등 여러 분야의 현안들을 논의하고 있다. 아시아의 개발불균형 해소를 위해서 활발하게 의견을 교환하면서 김영훈 회장은 국제사회의 평화정착과 균형 잡힌 인류사회의 발전을 위해 사명감을 가지고 회의에 참석하고 있다.

2005년 부산에서 열린 APEC에서는 부시 대통령과의 라운드테이블 대담을 가지며 고유가 정책에 대한 국제적 대안과 신재생에너지 공동연구에 대한 필요성을 토의하였다. 대성그룹 김영훈 회장은 이 대담에서 상호간의 협력을 도모해가자는 결론을 도출해 낸 바 있다.

한국을 대표하여 이러한 국제회의에 참석할 때마다 대성그룹 김영훈 회장이 느끼는 감회가 크다. 하나님께서 60년 전 아버지를 통해서 대성그룹을 일으키셨을 때, 아버지 개인과 한국의 역사적 상황은 심히 열악하였다. 어려운 상황 속에서 하나님께서는 신실하신 사랑으로 대성그룹을 눈동자 같이 지키시며 성장시키셨다. 이제 대성그룹은 명실공히 세계 초일류기업을 향해 나아가고 있다. 지금까지 60년 동안 은혜로 인도

9. Attendance at APEC Summit as Korean Business Representative

Annually, Chairman Younghoon David Kim attends the APEC Summit as the representative of Korean business in order to discuss various issues—energy, politics, economics, culture, environment, among others—with presidents and prime ministers of countries of the Asia-Pacific region, and with leading economic experts. Younghoon attends the summit with the mission to balance unequal development in Asia and to contribute to the advancement of civil city, via promotion of peaceful harmony and balance in the international community.

In 2005 at the APEC Summit held in Busan, Korea, Younghoon participated in a roundtable discussion with U.S. President George W. Bush. They discussed international measures and policies, as well as the need for cooperation in developing renewable energy resources. The roundtable discussion has led to further agreement for mutual cooperation in this area.

I see how honored Younghoon feels and how he gets quite emotional every time he represents Korea at international conventions. Sixty years ago when God raised the Daesung Group through our father, both Father's and Korea's situation was undeniably adverse. Despite the grave circumstances, God, in His faithful love, kept the Daesung Group as the

하신 하나님께서 앞으로 100주년을 기념하는 자리에 대성그룹이 설 때에 더욱 크고 놀라운 은혜를 찬양하게 하실 것을 믿는다.

우리의 모든 부족함에도 불구하고 오직 하나님께서 지극한 사랑과 은혜로 역사하시는 이유는 무엇일까? 바로 약한 자를 부르셔서 하나님의 능력을 나타내기 위함이시다. 대성의 역사는 은혜의 역사이다. 앞으로 대성의 나아갈 길에도 오직 은혜 위에 은혜가 역사할 것이라고 믿는다. 그러므로 대성그룹 모든 임직원들과 함께 이 민족과 열방이 예수 그리스도를 믿고 하나님의 은혜를 입어 하나님께 크게 쓰임 받기를 기도드린다.

일평생 아버지와 동행하신 하나님께서 이제 대성그룹 김영훈 회장과 모든 임직원들과 동행해 주심을 믿으며 말할 수 없는 은혜에 깊은 감사를 드린다. 대성그룹 김영훈 회장은 그의 자녀들에게도 하나님께서 임마누엘 되시어 저들과 함께 동행해 주시기를 바라며 믿음으로 기도드린다. 그들이 하나님의 은혜를 받고 국제사회 속에서 주님의 사랑과 공의를 나타내는 하나님의 용사로 자라기를 바라면서……

apple of His eye and raised it to where it stands today. Now, the Daesung Group is marching towards a position as a world-class global enterprise. I wait with great expectation for God, who had for the past six decades led the way in His grace, to lead the Group through to the 100th anniversary, when we will praise Him ever more for His even greater grace.

Why does God choose to fulfill His will through us, in spite of all our weaknesses, reliant only on His everlasting love and grace? He calls on the weak to carry out His will so that His power may be evident to all. The Daesung Group's history is one of pure grace. I trust that the road ahead will be showered with God's *Grace Upon Grace*. I pray for the day when all employees of the Daesung Group will—together with all peoples and nations—come to Christ in faith, wear the clothes of grace, and be used as vessels for God' s will.

I know that God, who walked with my father all throughout his life, is walking with Younghoon. I remain silent before Him and filled with deep thanksgiving for His grace. Younghoon prays in faith that God Emmanuel will also walk with his children. With hopes that his children will receive God's grace and grow as God's faithful soldiers, making His love and justice evident to all around the globe, Younghoon prays the following prayer:

대성그룹 김영훈 회장님이 자녀를 위하여 드리는 기도

하나님 아버지!

저희에게 예수님을 믿고 순종하며, 하나님 뜻을 행하며

하나님 일을 온전히 이루고자 하는

목마름과 배고픔을 주시옵소서.

저희 자녀들에게도 하나님의 뜻을 행하고자 하는

목마름을 허락하여 주시고

하나님 뜻을 온전히 이루고자 하는 배고픔을 허락하셔서

평생 열심으로 하나님 뜻을 행하며

열심으로 하나님 일을 이루게 하여 주시옵소서.

하나님 아버지!

저들이 힘을 합하여 하나가 천을 쫓고, 둘이 만을 쫓으며,

셋이 이 세상 모든 마귀를 다 멸하게 하여 주시옵소서.

다니엘과 그 친구들 같이 저희 자녀들도

선한 씨움을 필 싸우고

달려갈 길을 다 달리고 믿음을 지켜서

의의 면류관을 다 받게 해주시옵소서.

절대로 악에게 지지 말게 하시고 선으로 악을 이기는

**Chairman Younghoon David Kim's
Prayer for his Children**

Father God!

May we follow Jesus by faith.

May we thirst and hunger

to live for Your will and to fulfill Your purpose for us.

Instill in my children the thirst to live for Your will

and the hunger to fulfill Your purpose for them

so that they may wholeheartedly live for Your will

and wholeheartedly fulfill Your purpose.

Father God!

May my children unite so that

one may defeat a thousand; two, ten thousand;

and three, all that is wicked and displeasing to You.

May my children fight the good fight

as did Daniel and his friends.

May they finish their race, keep their faith,

and attain their crown of righteousness.

의의 용사가 다 되게 해주시옵소서.
우리 자녀들을 아버지여 복되게 하여 주시옵소서.
아브라함 같이 겸손하게 하나님과 동행하게 하시고
아브라함처럼 복 받게 하여 주시옵소서.

하나님 아버지 감사합니다.
겸손한 자를 찾으시고
하나님께 믿음으로 순종하는 자를 복 주시는
하나님 아버지!
'보라, 내가 열방을 유업으로 주리니
네 소유가 땅 끝까지 이르리라.' 하신 말씀을
오늘과 같이 이루어주시니 감사합니다.
저희 자녀들이 주 안에서 하나가 되어
오대양 육대주를 하나님 앞으로 돌이킬 수 있게 해
주시옵소서.
하나님의 지혜와 능력으로 오대양을 다스리게 하시고
하나님의 은혜와 진리로 육대주를 하나님께 돌이켜
하나님께 온전히 바치게 하시옵소서.
모든 열방이 하나님의 완전한 소유,
하나님의 영원한 소유, 하나님의 참된 소유가 되기를

May they never be defeated by their enemies but

become just and right soldiers who overcome evil with good.

Father, bless my children.

May they walk with You

with a humble heart like Abraham,

and may they receive the blessing of Abraham.

Father God, I thank you.

You call the humble

and bless those who follow you faithfully, Father God.

Thank you for remaining faithful to Your Word:

"Ask of me, and I will make

the nations your inheritance,

the ends of the earth your possession."

May my children become one in Christ and

bring the five oceans and six continents before You.

May we govern the five oceans

with Your wisdom and power,

and bring the six continents before You

with Your grace and truth—

간구하오며 다시 한 번 하나님의 놀라우신 은혜에

감사하옵고 예수 그리스도의 이름으로 기도드립니다. 아멘

all for Your glory.

May all the nations become Yours alone,

Yours for eternity, and Yours in spirit and in truth.

With thanksgiving for your amazing grace,

in Jesus' Name I pray.

Amen.

1979년 11월 10일

영훈에게.

그간 건강(健康) 하고 명랑하고 충실(充實)한 학창생활(學窓 生活)을 보내고 있을 줄 안다. 이곳 집 식구(食口) 들은 모다 건강(健康)하며 회사(會社)일도 잘 되어 가고 있으니 안심(安心)하여라. 일전(日前) 나의 생일(生日)에 대한 축하편지(祝賀便紙)를 잘 받아 보았다. 서울도 이제는 가을도 지나가고 초겨울의 계절(季節)이 되었네. 그 동안 높푸른 가을 하늘과 곱게 물들었던 단풍(丹楓)으로서 언제나 아름다운 한국(韓國)의 가을도 어느덧 지나가고 엄동(嚴冬)의 발자취가 다가온 감(感)이네. 지난 10월 26일 박정희 대통령(朴正熙 大統領)의 시해사건(弑害事件)은 국내외(國內外)에 걸쳐 비상(非常)한 충격(衝擊)을 주었다고 보네.

NOVEMBER 10, 1979

Dearest Younghoon,

I trust that you are enjoying a bright, healthy, purposeful life as a student. Rest assured, for the whole family is doing well and business is as good as usual. Thank you for sending me your heartfelt letter and birthday wishes. Autumn is now over and the winter season is approaching in Seoul. All too quickly have the high, blue autumn skies and the colorful fall leaves disappeared. Winter's footsteps seem to be coming our way.

The assassination of President Jung Hee Park on October 26 has drawn unusual attention from the international community and has shocked the entire world. I must say that Korea has responded quietly and calmly without causing the

그러나 그 후(後) 국내(國內)의 반응(反應)은 이 큰 충격(衝擊)을 자조(自助)와 침착(沈着)으로서 받아들여 하등(何等)의 혼란(混亂)이나 무질서(無秩序)를 나타냄이 없이 조용한 가운데 지내오고 있네. 사회질서(社會秩序)나 경제질서(經濟秩序)에 동요(動搖)의 기색(氣色)이 전혀 없고 오히려 교통사고(交通事故)나 범죄 등(犯罪 等)에서 평시(平時)보다 상당(相當)히 감소(減少)되는 현상(現像)이 나타나고 있네. 경제(經濟)의 기적적(奇績的) 확장(擴張)으로 세계(世界)의 이목(耳目)을 끈 한국(韓國)이 이번 사건(事件)을 계기(契機)로 해서 그간 잠재(潛在)되어 왔던 정치의식(政治意識)의 성장(成長)을 잘 나타내고 있다고 보겠네.

이번 사건(事件)의 불행(不幸)함은 말할 나위가 아니겠으나 그러나 앞으로 민주적(民主的) 방향(方向)으로 정치성장(政治成長)에 새로운 출발(出發)의 계기(契機)가 되어가고 있는 감(感)이네. 국내(國內)는 조용한 가운데 새 제도(制度), 질서(秩序)를 모색(摸索)하는 과정(課程)에 있으며 반드시 희망적(希望的)인 민주제도의 새 출발(出發)과 새로운 번영(繁榮)의 계제(階梯)를 밟아서 나갈 것을 확신(確信)할 수 있으니 아무쪼록 안심(安心)하고 열심(熱心)히 면학(勉學)에 힘써주기 바란다.

멀지 않아 학업(學業)을 마치고 조국발전(祖國發展)의 일군

slightest degree of chaos or disorder. The incident has not disturbed public order or the economic order. In fact, there have been fewer traffic accidents than usual and the crime rate has dropped. Korea has been drawing more and more international attention through the miraculous expansion of her economy, but I believe that this incident has now created the opportunity for the country to increase political awareness.

It is needless to say that the assassination of our president is a grave loss, but it seems this incident has triggered the start of the transformation of our government towards democracy. Korea is currently undergoing institutional reformation and searching for a new order. I am most certain that this phase of transformation will establish democratic systems and foster opportunities for unimaginable growth and prosperity. Be at ease and simply focus on your academic pursuits.

The time for your return home is fast approaching. I hope you set specific goals and spend the rest of your time equipping yourself to work for the good of your country. Also, I believe you have reached the age to establish your own household and march forward as an independent

으로서 돌아와야 될 것이니 확고(確固)한 목표(目標)를 세워서 나아가 주기 바란다. 그리고 빨리 장가도 가서 일가(一家)의 주인공(主人公)으로서 또 독립(獨立)된 사회인(社會人)으로서 나갈 날이 목전(目前)에 도래(到來)된 감(感)이로구나.

그럼 미시간의 추운 겨울이 다가오니 몸조심하고 더욱 건강(健康)하게 명랑(明朗)한 학창생활(學窓生活)을 보내주기 바란다. 그리고 한국(韓國)에 오고 싶은 생각(生覺)이 날 때는 언제나 돌아와서 고향(故鄕)에서 쉬다가 가도록 하여라. 그러면 오늘은 이만 줄인다.

아버지

member of the greater society. I hope you stay warm and healthy in the cold winter of Michigan, and that you continue to approach your studies with great joy and enthusiasm. If ever you feel like coming home, come and enjoy a brief time of relaxation.

I guess this is all for now.

YOUR FATHER

1981년 2월 12일

영훈(英薰)에게!

　그 동안 이곳은 오십 년(五十 年)만의 혹한(酷寒)에 예년에
보기 드문 엄청난 폭설(暴雪)로 산천(山川) 도시(都市) 할 것
없이 두터운 눈 속에 옴츠리고 지내오던 것이 겨우 1주일 전부
터 추위가 풀리기 시작하여 이제는 눈도 거의 다 녹아 없어지
고 불원(不遠) 다가올 봄 날씨를 연상(聯想)하리만큼 부드러운
기온(氣溫)으로 올라가고 있네.
　그간 여기 못지않게 추운 앤아보에서 여전히 몸 성하게 학
창생활(學窓生活)을 보내고 있을 줄 믿네. 이곳도 모두 건강(健
康) 하고 회사(會社)일도 별고(別故)없이 잘 지내고 있으니 안
심(安心)하여라.
　다만 그 동안 엄마가 원인(原因)모를 발열(發熱)로 38도 전
후로 소화불량(消化不良)으로 외출(外出)을 못한 채 정양(靜
養)하고 있다가 요 며칠 전부터 낫게 되어 오늘 새벽은 나와
같이 교회(敎會)도 나니왔네. 이제는 안심(安心)할 정도(定度)
로 회복(回復)하였으니 그렇게 알아라.
　그리고 지난 1월 28일부터 5일간 드볼트씨 부처(夫妻)와

Dearest Younghoon,

We had the heaviest snowfall in fifty years this winter. Cities and the countryside were covered with layers of snow. It has only been a week since the freezing temperatures finally began to rise again, melting most of the snow away and giving us a sense of the coming spring season.

I trust that you are doing well despite the bitter cold temperatures in Ann Arbor. Everyone back home is healthy and business is as usual, so do not worry about us.

Your mother had been struggling with indigestion and a fever that reached 38 degrees for a while, so she spent those days resting and recuperating at home. I am glad to say that she has been doing much better these past few days. She even joined me for early morning worship service today. Your mother is slowly recovering, so be at ease.

Mr. and Mrs. DeVault and their daughter Danielle stopped by in Korea on January 28th from their travels from Hong Kong, and for five days they toured around Seoul and Gyeongju. Our family expressed our hospitality and warm welcome to the DeVaults. We established a friendly relationship and they departed with a good impression of our

딸 다니엘 양이 홍콩여행 도중(道中)에 서울에 내방(來訪)하여 온 가족(家族) 전체(全體)의 열렬(熱烈)하고 융숭한 환영(歡迎)을 받고 닷새 동안 서울과 경주(慶州)를 구경하고 한국(韓國)과 우리 가정(家庭)에 대한 우정(友情)과 인상(印象)을 더욱 깊이 하고 돌아갔네. 드볼트씨 가족(家族)들은 퍽 즐겁고 만족(滿足)하였을 것으로 생각(生覺)되네.

어제는 영민(英民)이 집에서 새로 낳은 은혜(恩惠)의 백날로서 전가족(全家族)이 모여서 즐거운 백날 잔치를 기졌네.

국내(國內)도 이제 점차로 질서(秩序)가 잘 잡혀 가고 정치(政治), 경제(經濟), 사회(社會) 전반(全般)에 걸쳐서 새로운 광명(光明)이 비추어 오는 느낌이며 새로운 발전(發展)과 전진(轉進)이 곧 시작(始作)되겠네.

그리고 29회 생일(生日)을 축하(祝賀)한다. 타국(他國)에서 혼자 맞이하는 생일(生日)이나마 이곳 가족(家族)들은 마음으로 축하(祝賀)를 보내고 있네. 그러면 오늘은 이만하고 마치겠네.

아버지

family. I believe they enjoyed their stay with us.

The entire family gathered yesterday at Young Min's home to celebrate the hundredth-day party of their new bundle of joy, Grace.

Order is gradually being restored in Korea, including political, economic, and social order as a whole. I believe that the future prospects for this country look bright and that we will soon experience new growth and development.

I want to wish you a happy 29th birthday. The family sends their heartfelt birthday wishes to you in hopes that your birthday away from home may be celebrated with joy.

I guess this is all for now.

YOUR FATHER

1981년 8월 14일

영훈(英薰)에게!

마닐라에 무사(無事)히 도착(到着)하여 업무훈련(業務訓鍊) 과정(課程)에 들어가게 되었다 하니 반갑게 생각한다.

그리고 그간 여름은 보스톤에서 정주(晶珠)누나와 즐거운 여름을 지나면서 독서(讀書)와 사색(思索)으로서 충실한 시간(時間)을 보내었다 하니 젊은 시절에 가장 알찬 장래(將來)를 여러 가지 구상(具象)하고 설계(設計)하는데 퍽이나 유익(有益)하였을 것으로 믿는다.

이곳은 지금 혹한(酷寒)에 이은 폭서(暴暑)의 여름으로서 괴로운 삼복(三伏)이었으나 이제는 낮에는 30도를 넘는 더위이나 아침 저녁은 서늘해져서 가을이 먼 발치나마 다가선 느낌이네.

그 동안 나는 엄마와 정한(正韓)이 하고 설악(雪岳)산에 일주일 다녀오면서 여름 바캉스답게 잘 쉬었네.

영민이도 일주간 휴가(休暇)중이고, 너의 큰 형은 8월 15일 역시 설악(雪岳)으로 휴가(休暇)로 떠난다고 하네.

이곳 모두 건강하게 지내고 있으며 영주 가족 모두 건강히게 즐겁게 지내고 있네. 끝으로 너의 건강과 즐거운 훈련(訓鍊)기가 되기를 기원(起源)한다.

아버지

AUGUST 14, 1981

Dearest Younghoon,

I am glad to hear that you have safely arrived and commenced training in Manila. I trust that your summer in Boston with your older sister Jung Joo was spent joyfully and productively, reading books and preparing for a highly prosperous future.

Following the bitter cold winter season, we have been enduring intense heat, as it is the hottest period of the summer. But I am relieved to say that although the daytime temperatures reach above 30 degrees, the morning and evening breeze feels cool. It seems like autumn is just around the corner. Your mother, Jung Han, and I went on a one week summer vacation to Mt. Sorak. Young Min is away on vacation for a week, and your eldest brother Young Tae says he will go on vacation to Mt. Sorak on August 15.

We are all doing well and Young Joo's family is also very healthy and happy. I wish you good health and hope that the remainder of your time in training is pleasant.

YOUR FATHER

　아버지께서 소천하신 후, 나는 아버지의 생애를 전기로 남기고 싶었다. 아버지의 삶과 아버지가 이룩하신 대성그룹 60년 역사를 정리하여, 대성그룹에 나타내신 하나님의 은혜를 바르게 이해하고 전해야 하겠다고 느꼈기 때문이다. 이제 그 첫 프로젝트로 아버지 회고록의 편집을 마치면서 아버지와 대성그룹에 처음부터 지금까지 신실하신 사랑으로 함께하신 하나님께 모든 영광을 돌린다.

　나는 아버지의 생애와 대성그룹 60년 역사를 되돌아 보며 정리하는 과정에서 말할 수 없이 큰 기쁨과 감격을 느꼈다. 그 모든 과정에서 천국에 계신 아버지께서 매우 기뻐하고 계심을 계속 확신할 수 있었다. 일생 동안 진실하게 살기 위해 노력하신 아버지의 수고 뒤에 숨어 있는 하나님의 은혜에 대한 감사와 찬양이 내 마음 깊이 솟아 나왔다. 고생하시던 어린 시절부터 성공하셔서 한국 에너지산업계를 대표하시기까지, 그리고 김영훈 회장님에게 대성그룹을 물려주시고 하나님 나라를 소망하시며 주님 앞에 가실 준비를 하실 때까지, 우리의 주가 되시는 예수님은 아버지의 손을 한시도 놓지 않으셨음을 보았다. 나는 아버지 가까이서 아버지의 강하심과 약하심을 모두

Ever since Father passed away, I have been meaning to write a biography of his life. I felt a pressing desire to share the countless blessings that God showered down throughout both the company's history and my father's life. As I have finally reached the end of editing my father's memoir, I give all praise and glory to God Who, through His faithfulness and unchanging love, watched over my father since the founding days of the Daesung Group.

I experienced unspeakable joy and inspiration while flipping through my father's memories and the history of the Daesung Group. In making this compilation of my father's words, I imagined him looking down at me from heaven, smiling ever so joyously. Overflowing from within me was a heart of thanksgiving for God's grace which stood behind my father's every move and honest heart of gold. Jesus tightly held onto my father's hands and never once let go. Even during his tough childhood and up to his success as a representing figure in the Korean energy industry; even when he released his grip on the Daesung Group and named Younghoon the new chairman; and even when he, with great hopes for God's kingdom, was preparing to be with the Lord, God never let go. Because I had seen my father's strengths

보았기에 아버지를 끝까지 붙드신 주님의 용서의 손, 사랑의 손, 은혜의 손에 대한 감사를 고백하지 않을 수 없다.

지금 아버지가 천국에서 누리는 기쁨은 전적으로 하나님의 은혜로 말미암은 것이다. 죄인의 괴수라고 스스로 고백한 바울처럼 전적으로 타락한 우리 인생이 어떻게 거룩한 하나님의 존전에 나아갈 수 있겠는가? 불가능한 일이다. 오직 하나님의 외아들 예수 그리스도께서 인간의 몸을 입고 이 땅에 오셔서 우리 죄를 용서해 주시려고 그 피를 다 쏟으심으로 가능케 하셨다. 죽으신 지 사흘 만에 예수님은 다시 살아나시고 승천하셔서 하늘과 땅의 모든 권세를 가지고 다스리고 계신다. 하나님의 택하심을 받아 누구든지 예수 그리스도를 믿기만 하면 하나님의 자녀가 되어 영원한 생명을 누리게 하신다. 이것이 아버지 김수근 회장님이 받으신 은혜이다. 이 책을 읽는 모든 분들도 그리스도를 믿고 영생을 받는 축복을 받으시기를 기도드린다.

아버지께서 들려주신 이 회고록의 부제는 '천국에 가신 아버지가 자녀들에게 남겨주신 이야기'가 되어야 할 것 같다. 헨델은 메시아를 작곡할 때 몇 주 되시 않는 짧은 시간에 영원히 남을 대곡을 썼다. 하나님의 영감으로 쓸 때만이 가능한 일이다. 지난 몇 달 동안 대성그룹의 60년 역사를 정리하면서 놀

and weaknesses from up close, I cannot help but give thanksgiving for God's forgiving, loving, gracious hand that held my father's hands.

The joy my father now experiences in heaven is solely on account of God's grace. Like Paul, who confessed on his own accord that he was a sinner, how can we who are sinners ever set foot in our holy God's house? This is impossible. But it was made possible through the blood of God's only begotten Son, Jesus Christ, who was sent in human form and who died on the cross for our sins. Jesus rose from the dead on the third day and reigns over heaven and earth. Whoever turns his ear to God's calling and believes in Christ, he becomes a child of God and will live eternally. This is the grace that my father received. I pray that all who read this book may believe in Christ and receive the blessing of eternal life.

I think the most suitable subtitle for my father's memoir is "A Father's Words to His Children from Heaven." Handel's *Messiah* was completed in a matter of weeks, but it will remain forever as one of the greatest works of all time. Such a great work cannot come into existence without God's providence. I tasted a bit of heaven's joy while reminiscing through the Daesung Group's sixty-year history over the last few months. I was able to sense the peace, joy, and thanksgiving that my father feels right now, living in the holy kingdom of our gracious, faithful God. I can hear God say,

라운 천국의 기쁨을 맛보았다. 글을 정리하는 동안 인자하심과 신실하심으로 아버지를 평생 선대하신 하나님 존전에서 평안과 기쁨과 감사와 감격가운데 계신 아버지의 마음을 느낄 수 있었다. 못 자국 난 손으로 나의 아버지를 평생 붙드시고 긍휼 가운데 은혜로 이끄신 우리 주 예수 그리스도께서 이제 아버지를 품에 안으시고 "내가 그 모든 것을 다 이루었다."고 말씀하시는 음성을 듣는다. 그러므로 김수근 회장님의 삶과 대성그룹의 60년사는 한마디로 하나님의 역사요, 은혜 위에 은혜임을 증거한다. 또한 이러한 놀라우신 하나님의 은혜가 100년 대성의 비전을 반드시 이루게 하실 줄로 믿는다.

> "우리가 다 그의 충만한데서 받으니
> 은혜 위에 은혜러라"
> (요한복음 1:16)

2007년 5월 10일 대성그룹 창립 60주년을 맞이하며
연세대학교 교수 / 대성닷컴 사장
김정주 박사

"It was I who made all these things possible," as Jesus, Who held my father for a lifetime with His nail-scarred hands and Who led my father with grace and compassion, embraces my father. Founding Chairman of the Daesung Group Soo Keun Kim's life and this 60th anniversary special publication are both a part of God's history and proof of His *Grace Upon Grace*. I know that God, with His amazing grace, will carry out His work through the Daesung Group and guide the way towards the Group's 100th anniversary vision.

> [16]*And from His fullness have we all received,*
> *Grace Upon Grace.*
> *John 1:16 (RSV)*

Dr. Jung Joo Kim
Professor, Yonsei University
President, Daesung.com
In celebration of the 60th anniversary of the Daesung Group
May 10, 2007

● **창업주 김수근 대성그룹 회장 약력**

약 력

출생지: 대구

생년월일: 1916년 8월 28일 (음력)

1929 – 1934	대구상업고등학교
1940 – 1943	일본니혼대학교 법학 학사
1995	연세대학교 명예박사
1944. 8 – 1945	경북실령금융조합 이사
1945. 11 – 1946	경북영천금융조합 이사
1947. 5	대성산업공사 창립, 대표이사
1952 – 1964	경북석탄조합 이사장
1957. 10	대성연탄 창립, 대표이사
1964	탄광협회 부회장
1964 – 1968	프로판가스협회 회장
1965. 6	대성탄좌개발 창립, 대표이사
1965. 7	대한광업회 이사
1968. 7	대성산업 창립, 대표이사
1969	석유협회 부회장
1973. 6	전국경제인연합회 이사

- ### *About Founding Chairman of the Daesung Group*
  ### *Soo Keun Kim*

BACKGROUND

28 August 1916	Born in Daegu, Korea
1929-1934	Daegu Commerical High School
1940-1943	Bachelor of Law, Nihon University, Japan
1995	Honorary Doctor, Yonsei University, Korea
August 1944-1945	Director, Gyeongbuk Sillyeong Farmers' Bank
November 1945-1946	Director, Gyeongbuk Yeongcheon Farmers' Bank
May 1947	Founded Daesung Industrial Corporation
1952-1964	Executive Director, Gyeongbuk Coal Association
October 1957	Founded Daesung Briquette Co., Ltd.
1964	Vice Chairman, Coal Mine Association
1964-1968	Chairman, Propane Gas Association
June 1965	Founded Daesung Consolidated Coal Mining Co., Ltd.
July 1965	Director, Mining Association of Korea
July 1968	Founded Daesung Industrial Co., Ltd.
1969	Vice Chairman, Korea Petroleum Association
June 1973	Director, Federation of Korean Industries (FKI)

1976. 6   대성광업개발 창립, 대표이사
1976. 7   창원기화기공업 창립, 대표이사
1979. 2 – 1985   대성산소 대표이사
1980. 9   대한석탄협회 부회장
1981. 2   대성산업 대표이사 회장
1981. 2 – 1990   민정당후원회 부회장

1982. 4   한국장애자재활협회 부회장

1982. 5   제11대 서울상공회의소 상임의원

1983   대성그룹 회장
1983. 11   서울도시가스 창립, 대표이사 회장
                                 대구도시가스 창립, 대표이사 회장
1987. 2   한국도시가스협회 회장
1990   민자당후원회 회장
                                 신한국당 재정위원회 부위원장

1995   경기장학회 이사장
1995. 6   1998   전국성세인연합회
                                 남북경협특별위원회 위원

June 1976	Founded Daesung Mining Development Co., Ltd.
July 1976	Founded Changwon Carburetor Industrial Co., Ltd.
February 1979-1985	Chairman, Daesung Oxyton Co., Ltd.
September 1980	Vice Chairman, Korea Coal Association
February 1981	CEO & Chairman, Daesung Industrial Co., Ltd.
February 1981-1990	Vice Chairman, Democratic Justice Party Support Association
April 1982	Vice Chairman, Korea Society for Rehabilitation of the Disabled
May 1982	Permanent Member, Seoul Chamber of Commerce and Industry
1983	Chairman, Daesung Group
November 1983	Founded Seoul City Gas Co., Ltd.
	Founded Daegu City Gas Co., Ltd.
February 1987	Chairman, Korea City Gas Association
1990	Chairman, Democratic Justice Party Support Association
	Vice Chairman, Financial Committee of the New Korea Party
1995	Chief Director, Kyunggi Scholarship Society
June 1995-1996	Committee Member, the Foundation of Korean Industries — South-North Joint Economic Cooperation Steering Committee

| 1997. 10 | (재)해강과학문화재단 설립,이사장 |
| 2000. 11 | 대성그룹 명예회장 |

수상 경력

1967. 4	국무총리 무연탄증산 공로표창
1977. 3	산업포장
1983. 3	은탑산업훈장
1988	프랑스 경제발전 공로훈장
1999. 3. 17	제26회 상공의 날 금탑산업훈장

October 1997	Chief Director/Founder, Daesung Haegang
	Science and Culture Foundation
November 2000	Honorary Chairman, Daesung Group

AWARDS

April 1967	Prime Minister's Award of Excellence in
	Coal Production
March 1977	Industry Medal
March 1983	Silver Tower Industrial Medal of Honor
1988	France Economic Development Honor
	(La Legion d'honneur)
17 March 1999	Golden Tower Industrial Medal of Honor
	(Commerce Day)

● 김영훈 대성그룹 회장 약력

출생지: 대구

생년월일: 1952년 2월 29일

학력

1968 - 1971   경기고등학교
1971 - 1975   서울대학교 법대 행정학과

1977 - 1981   미시간대학교대학원 법학 석사
                       (MCL), 경영학 석사 (MBA)

1983 - 1984   하버드대학교 대학원 국제경제학

1984 - 1987   하버드대학교 대학원 신학석사
                       (MDiv)

약력

1981 - 1983   Citibank Seoul, Assistant Manager
1988 - 1993   대성산업㈜ 상무이사

- ***About Chairman of the Daesung Group***
  Younghoon David Kim

29 February 1952   Born in Daegu, Korea

EDUCATION

1968-1971   Kyunggi High School

1971-1975   Seoul National University

         BA in Law and Public Administration

1977-1981   University of Michigan Graduate School

         Master of Business Administration (MBA)

         Master of Comparative Law (MCL)

1983-1984   Harvard University Graduate School of Arts and Sciences

         International Economics

1984-1987   Harvard Divinity School

         Master of Divinity (MDiv)

BACKGROUND

1981-1983   Assistant Manager, Citibank Seoul

1988-1993   Executive Director, Daesung Industrial Co., Ltd.

1990 – 1993	창원기화기공업㈜ 상무이사, 대성그룹 본부 상무이사
1995 – 1997	대성그룹 본부 부사장
1997 – 2000	대성그룹 기획조정실장 사장 창원기화기 공업㈜ 대표이사 사장 대성정기㈜ 대표이사 사장
1997 – 2001	대성산업㈜ 대표이사 사장 경북도시가스㈜ 대표이사 사장
1997 – 2003	대구 TRS㈜ 대표이사 사장
1997 – 2005	㈜한국케이블 TV 경기방송 회장
2001 – 현재	대성그룹 회장 글로리아 트레이딩㈜, 시나이미디어㈜, 알앤알건설㈜, 경북도시가스㈜ 대표이사 회장
2002 – 현재	바이넥스트창업투자 ㈜, 대성닷컴㈜ 대표이사 회장
2003 – 현재	대성글로벌네트웍㈜, Acts 투자자문 ㈜, 알파정보통신㈜, 베타정보통신㈜, 감마정보통신, 델타정보통신㈜, 오메가정보통신㈜ 대표이사 회장

1990-1993	Executive Director, Changwon Carburetor Industrial Co., Ltd.
	Executive Director, Daesung Group
1995-1997	Vice President, Daesung Group
1997-2000	President, Daesung Group Office of Planning & Administration
	President, Changwon Carburetor Industrial Co., Ltd.
	President, Daesung Automotive Co., Ltd.
1997-2001	President, Daesung Industrial Co., Ltd.
	President, Gyeongbuk City Gas Co., Ltd.
1997-2003	Chairman & CEO, Daegu TRS Co., Ltd.
1997-2005	Chairman & CEO, Kyounggi Cable TV, Ltd.
2001-present	Chairman & CEO
	Daesung Group
	Gloria Trading Co., Ltd.
	Sinai Media Co., Ltd.
	RNR Engineering & Construction Co., Ltd.
2002-present	Chairman & CEO
	BiNEXT CAPiTAL Co., Ltd.,
	Daesung.com Co., Ltd.,
2003-present	Chairman & CEO
	Daesung Global Network Co., Ltd.,
	Acts Capital Management Co., Ltd.,
	Alpha Telecommunication Co., Ltd.,
	Beta Telecommunication Co., Ltd.,

2006 - 현재   코리아닷컴 커뮤니케이션
                    대표이사 회장

Gamma Telecommunication Co., Ltd.,

Delta Telecommunication Co., Ltd.,

Omega Telecommunication Co., Ltd.

Chairman & CEO, Korea.com Communications Co., Ltd.

2006-present

● 김영훈 대성그룹 회장 대외 경력

1997 - 1998	서울충정로타리 클럽 초대회장
1998 - 1999	Chairman, Gas Session in APEC Energy Ministers' Conference
1998 - 현재	사랑의 집짓기 운동연합회 한국본부 이사
1999 - 현재	전국경제인 연합회 이사 APEC 기업 자문위원
2000 - 현재	한·몽 경제협력위원회 위원장
2001 - 현재	주한 몽골 명예영사
2001. 12 - 2003	한국위험통제학회 부회장
2002. 3 - 현재	한국능률협회 부회장 (비상근)
2002. 4 - 현재	한국도시가스협회 회장 APEC 산하 PEG (Partnership for Equitable Growth) 위원회 회장
2002. 9 - 현재	ASEM 산하 AEBF(Asia-Europe Business Forum) 한국위원
2002. 12 - 현재	한·미 재계회의 한국위원
2003. 4 - 현재	한국자원경제학회 부회장 전경련 동북아 특별위원회 위원

ACTIVITIES

1997-1998	Founder & First President, Chungjung Rotary Club in Seoul
1998-1999	Chairman, Gas Session in APEC Energy Ministers' Conference
1998-present	Board Member, Habitat for Humanity Korea
1999-present	Executive Director, Federation of Korean Industries (FKI)
	Committee Member, APEC Business Advisory council
2000-present	Chairman, Korea-Mongolia Economic Cooperation Committee
2001-present	Honorary Consul of Mongolia
December 2001-2003	Vice President, Korea Society of Risk Governance (KOSRIG)
March 2002-present	Vice President, Korea Management Association
April 2002-present	Chairman, Korea City Gas Association
	Chairman, APEC Partnership for Equitable Growth (PEG)
September 2002-present	Korea Representative, ASEM Asia-Europe Business Forum (AEBF)
December 2002-present	Korea Representative, Korea-U.S. Business Council
April 2003-present	Vice President, Korea Environmental Economics Association
	Board Member, Federation of Korean Industries (FKI) —Special Committee on North-East Asia

2004. 1 – 현재	한국위험통제학회 감사
	전경련 문화산업특별위원회 위원장
2005. 1 – 현재	서울산업대학교 에너지환경대학원 명예대학원장
2005. 2 – 현재	제9대 대구육상경기연맹 회장
2005. 9 – 현재	World Energy Council 부회장

● 김영훈 대성그룹 회장 홈페이지_ www.younghoonkim.com

January 2004–present	Auditor, Korea Society of Risk Governance (KOSRIG)
	Chairman, Federation of Korean Industries (FKI) —Special Committee on the Culture Industry
January 2005–present	Honorary Dean, Seoul National University of Technology Graduate School of Energy and Environment
February 2005–present	President, Daegu Track and Field League
September 2005–present	Vice Chairman, World Energy Council

● 대성그룹 연혁

1947. 5. 10	대성산업공사 창립
1959. 9. 18	대성연탄주식회사 설립,
	왕십리공장 준공
1960. 7. 10	문경탄광 인수
1965. 6. 1	대성탄좌개발주식회사 설립
1968. 7. 4	대성산업주식회사 설립
1969. 6. 3	대성와사공업주식회사 설립
1970. 10. 26	영등포공장 준공
1971. 6. 30	대성산업, 대성와사공업 합병
1972. 6. 30	대성산업, 대성연탄과 대성산업공사 합병
1976. 6. 25	대성광업개발주식회사 설립
1976. 7. 19	창원기화기공업주식회사 설립
1979. 2. 19	대성산소주식회사 설립

10 May 1947	Daesung Industrial Corporation founded
18 September 1959	Daesung Briquette Co., Ltd., established & construction of coal briquette plant in Wangsimni completed
10 July 1960	Takes over the Mungyeong Coal Mine
1 June 1965	Daesung Consolidated Coal Mining Co., Ltd., established
4 July 1968	Daesung Industrial Co., Ltd., established
3 June 1969	Daesung Wasa Co., Ltd., established
26 October 1970	Construction of coal briquette plant in Yeongdeungpo completed
30 June 1971	Daesung Industrial Co., Ltd., & Daesung Wasa Co., Ltd., merge
30 June 1972	Daesung Industrial Co., Ltd., & Daesung Briquette Co., Ltd., & Daesung Industrial Corporation merge
25 June 1976	Daesung Mining Development Co., Ltd., established
19 July 1976	Changwon Carburetor Industrial Co., Ltd., established
19 February 1979	Daesung Oxyton Co., Ltd., established

1980. 11. 19	대성호주현지법인 설립
1982. 3. 25	대성미국현지법인 설립
1982. 11. 19	대성홍콩현지법인 설립
1983. 1. 31	대구도시가스주식회사 설립
1983. 11. 28	서울도시가스주식회사 설립
1985. 8. 21	한국캠브리지필터주식회사 설립
1985. 9. 19	대성쎌틱주식회사 설립
1985. 10. 2	문경새재관광주식회사 설립
1987. 6. 25	대성정기주식회사 설립
1987. 12. 30	대성계전주식회사 설립
1988. 3. 5	대성타코주식회사 설립
1988. 5. 17	대성나찌유압공업주식회사 설립
1989. 7. 23	대성캐나다현지법인 설립
1989. 9. 11	대성헨켈화학주식회사 설립
1989. 10. 10	대성에너지기기주식회사 설립
1989. 11. 15	대성산업 건설사업부 발족
1990. 12. 24	주식회사 성주인디내셔날 설립
1992. 7. 8	대구도시가스엔지니어링주식회사 설립
1993. 8. 30	서울도시가스엔지니어링주식회사 설립
1994. 3. 18	대성탄좌개발, 대성자원주식회사로 상호 변경

19 November 1980	Daesung Australia Pty., Ltd., established
25 March 1982	Daesung America Co., Inc., established in New York
19 November 1982	Daesung Hong Kong Co., Inc., established
31 January 1983	Daegu City Gas Co., Ltd., established
28 November 1983	Seoul City Gas Co., Ltd., established
21 August 1985	Cambridge Filter Korea Co., Ltd., established
19 September 1985	Daesung Chaffoteaux et Maury Co., Ltd., established
2 October 1985	Mungyeong Saejae Tour Co., Ltd., established
25 June 1987	Daesung Automotive Co., Ltd., established
30 December 1987	Daesung Measuring Co., Ltd., established
5 March 1988	Daesung Taco Co., Ltd., established
17 May 1988	Daesung Nachi Hydraulic Co., Ltd., established
23 July 1989	Daesung Canada Inc. established
11 September 1989	Daesung Henkel Chemical Co., Ltd., established
10 October 1989	Daesung Energy Appliance Co., Ltd., established
15 November 1989	Daesung Industrial Co., Ltd.—construction business division added
24 December 1990	Sungjoo International Co., Ltd.,established
8 July 1992	Daegu City Gas Engineering Co., Ltd., established
30 August 1993	Seoul City Gas Engineering Co., Ltd., established
18 March 1994	Daesung Consolidated Coal Mining Co., Ltd., renamed Daesung Resources Co., Ltd.

1996. 7. 5	관훈동사옥 매입
1996. 7. 10	대구TRS주식회사 설립
1997. 7. 4	㈜한국케이블TV 경기방송 설립
1997. 7. 12	경북도시가스주식회사 설립
1997. 8. 1	대성산업이 대성자원 흡수합병
1999. 1. 1	서울에너지주식회사 설립
2000. 7. 11	창원기화기공업주식회사, 대성정기주식회사 계열분리
2001. 6. 30	대성그룹이 대성산업군, 서울도시가스군, 대구도시가스군의 3개군으로 분리
2001. 8. 10	주식회사 성주인터내셔날 계열분리
2001. 12. 19	알앤알리모델링㈜ 설립
2001. 12. 19	글로리아트래이딩㈜ 설립
2002. 1. 2	시나이미디어㈜ 설립
2002. 1. 4	대구TRS㈜ 가 대구도시가스ENG㈜ 흡수 합병
2002. 4. 24	대성해강과학문화재단 설립

5 July 1996	Gwanhun-dong Building purchased
10 July 1996	Daegu TRS Co., Ltd., established
4 July 1997	Korea Cable Television Gyeonggi Center Co., Ltd., established
12 July 1997	Gyeongbuk City Gas Co., Ltd., established
1 August 1997	Daesung Resources Co., Ltd., & Daesung Industrial Co., Ltd., merge
1 January 1999	Seoul Energy Co., Ltd., established
11 July 2000	Changwon Carburetor Industrial Co., Ltd., & Daesung Automotive Co., Ltd., separate from the Daesung Group
30 June 2001	The Daesung Group separates into three major divisions: Daesung Industrial, Seoul City Gas, and Daegu City Gas
10 August 2001	Sungjoo International Co., Ltd., separates from the Daesung Group
19 December 2001	R&R Remodeling Co., Ltd., established
19 December 2001	Gloria Trading Co., Ltd., established
2 January 2002	Sinai Media Co., Ltd., established
4 January 2002	Daegu TRS Co., Ltd., & Daegu City Gas Engineering Co., Ltd., merge
24 April 2002	Daesung Haegang Science and Culture Foundation established

2002. 5. 10	대성청정에너지연구소 개소
2002. 6. 4	대구은행 계열의 창투사인 인사이트벤처
	인수하여 BiNEXT HiTEC로 사명 변경
2002. 11. 20	대성닷컴㈜ 설립
2002. 12. 18	대성차이나㈜ 설립
2003. 1	대성싱가폴㈜ 설립
2003. 5. 16	알파정보통신㈜, 베타정보통신㈜,
	감마정보통신㈜, 델타정보통신㈜,
	오메가정보통신㈜ 설립
2003. 6. 18	대성글로벌네트웍㈜ 설립
2003. 9. 2	액츠투자자문㈜ 계열사 편입
2003. 12. 26	㈜내일네트워크 계열사 편입
2004. 5. 24	대구에너지환경㈜ 설립
2005. 3. 15	바이넥스트하이테크㈜를
	바이넥스트창업투자㈜로 사명 변경
2005. 7. 7	대성글로벌네트웍(주) 대구 남산동
	컨택센터 개관
2006. 1. 20	(주)코리아닷컴커뮤니케이션즈 인수

10 May 2002	Daesung Institute for Clean Energy established
4 June 2002	The Daesung Group undertakes Insight Ventures Corp., an affiliate enterprise of Daegu Bank Ltd. Insight Venture is renamed BiNEXT HiTEC Co., Ltd.
20 November 2002	Daesung.com Co., Ltd., established
18 December 2002	Daesung China Co., Ltd., established
January 2003	Daesung Singapore Co., Ltd., established
16 May 2003	Alpha Telecommunication Co., Ltd., established
	Beta Telecommunication Co., Ltd., established
	Gamma Telecommunication Co., Ltd., established
	Delta Telecommunication Co., Ltd., established
	Omega Telecommunication Co., Ltd., established
18 June 2003	Daesung Global Network Co., Ltd., established
2 September 2003	Acts Capital Management Co., Ltd., incorporated
26 December 2003	Naeil Network Co., Ltd., incorporated
24 May 2004	Daegu Energy & Environment Co., Ltd., established
15 March 2005	BiNEXT HiTEC Co., Ltd., renamed BiNEXT CAPiTAL Co., Ltd.
7 July 2005	Daesung Global Network Co., Ltd., opens Contact Center in Daegu
20 January 2006	Korea.com Communications acquired

| 2007. 1. 5 | 알앤알리모델링㈜를 알앤알건설㈜로 |
| | 사명 변경 |

● 대성그룹 홈페이지_www.daesung.com

5 January 2007   R&R Remodeling Co., Ltd. is renamed

                        RNR Engineering & Construction

은혜 위에 은혜

초판 인쇄 | 2007년 5월 1일
초판 발행 | 2007년 5월 10일

발행처 | 대성닷컴(주) JCR
발행인 | 김영훈

등록번호 | 제300-2003-82호
등록일자 | 2003년 5월 6일

서울시 종로구 관훈동 151-8 동덕빌딩 11층 대성닷컴(주)
대표전화 | (02)3700-1764
팩스 | (02)3700-1701
www.daesungbook.com   jcrbooks@korea.com

ISBN 978-89-958974-2-3(04230)
ISBN 978-89-958974-4-7(세트)
ⓒ 대성닷컴(주) JCR 2007

정가 9,500원

본서에 인용한 성경 본문은 특별한 표기가 없는 한 성경전서 개역개정판을 사용하였습니다.

Grace Upon Grace

JCR, DAESUNG.COM CO., LTD.
11th fl. Dongduk Bldg. 151-8 Gwanhun-dong Jongno-gu
Seoul, 110-300 Korea
Tel +82 2 3700 1764   Fax +82 2 3700 1701
www.daesungbook.com   jcrbooks@korea.com

ISBN 978-89-958974-2-3(04230)
ISBN 978-89-958974-4-7(Set)
ⓒ Daesung.com Co., Ltd., JCR 2007

All Scripture is taken from the New International Version (NIV) unless otherwise stated.

Printed in Korea